GRADES 3–5

Teaching Students to Read
Informational Texts—
Independently

CCSS
SUPPORTS THE COMMON CORE STATE STANDARDS

NANCY L. WITHERELL

Edited by Lynne Wilson
Supervising Editor: Mela Ottaiano
Acquiring Editor: Joanna Davis-Swing
Cover design by Brian LaRossa
Interior design by Melinda Belter
Cover photos by Czamfir/Big Stock Photo (Boy), Liang Zhang/Big Stock Photo (Flowers), JohanSwanepoel/Big Stock Photo (Earth), Kletr/Big Stock Photo (Giraffe), AlexMax/Big Stock Photo (U.S. Flag), xaoc/Big Stock Photo (Hot Air Balloon)
Interior illustrations by Teresa Anderko
ISBN: 978-0-545-55491-6
Copyright © 2014 by Nancy L. Witherell
Illustrations copyright © 2014 by Scholastic Inc.
All rights reserved.
Published by Scholastic Inc.
Printed in the U.S.A.

1 2 3 4 5 6 7 8 9 10   40   21 20 19 18 17 16 15 14

New York · Toronto · London · Auckland · Sydney
Mexico City · New Delhi · Hong Kong · Buenos Aires

Teaching *Resources*

Table of Contents

Introduction

Every day, teachers ask students questions about what they have just read. How many times have you asked a question to students and received a blank-eyed response? Yet they have just finished reading—you watched them! Most of them have read the whole assigned text—word by word, but something went wrong somewhere. Many of these students just didn't interact with the text enough to fully comprehend or retain the information.

The strategies and activities presented in this book are meant to help students engage with text, comprehend more fully, and retain the information—*independently of the teacher*. This is not a book about "independent reading" in the general sense because it deals with assigned reading, which is essentially limited-choice reading. Students may read silently on their own, or work with a partner, without depending on your help.

Lessons within this book teach students various navigational techniques for reading and interacting with the text. Students learn to look at text features and text structure to aid them in their understanding. Each set of instructional steps is based on Pearson's Gradual Release of Responsibility Model (Pearson and Gallagher, 1983). In this model, the work of the strategy is initially on the teacher as you demonstrate and explain how a strategy is to be done. Next, during the guided practice phase, the teacher supports students as they help in completing the strategy. The goal is to prepare students to perform the strategy independently.

These lessons are also differentiated to provide support for students at all levels. As students read, interact with the information from the text, and work with the material in various ways, they will be more apt to store the information in their long-term memory for retrieval when needed.

The strategies and activities in this book align with the Common Core State Standards (CCSS) for grades 3, 4, and 5. Each lesson focuses on a particular standard, although many of the activities can be used or adapted to meet a number of the Common Core State Standards. The lessons in the first section cover the anchor standards for Key Ideas and Details. Those in the second section focus on Craft and Structure. The third section's lessons center on Integration of Knowledge and Ideas. For an overview of the standards covered in each lesson, refer to the Connections to the Common Core State Standards grid on page 5 and the Meeting the Common Core bursts throughout the book. For more information about the CCSS, visit the following Web site: www.corestandards.org/the-standards/.

Each lesson contains the following sections:

 The **Meeting the Common Core** burst lists the primary English Language Arts Common Core State Standard that is being targeted during the lesson and by using the strategy. (All of the lessons will help students meet Standard 10, reading and comprehending grade-level informational texts independently and proficiently.)

What Is It? explains the strategy and gives an overview of how it is done.

 Why Use It? evidences that the strategy is formed from effective practices and based on research, which supports the strategy's usefulness in engaging students in their reading.

 The **Text Selection** section gives tips on how to choose the right text for this strategy. For many of the lessons, any well-written informational text at the students' independent reading level will work. But for some of the strategies, such as using the Compare and Contrast graphic organizer, it is important to select the text carefully.

 The **Instructional Steps** give clear, step-by-step directions to help you get students to use the strategy successfully on their own. These steps are divided into three sections: Introduction, Teacher Modeling and Guided Practice, and Directions for Independent Application. Following the steps gradually releases the responsibility of the strategy to students, either as a solo activity or with a partner.

The **Strategy in Action** gives an example of the activity. It includes sample text to use with the class as you model the strategy. In many chapters, we've given additional modeling examples.

 Taking Ownership allows students to work with the information from the text one more time. This task is meant to provide another review and application of the material to aid students in their retention of the information. The task may be a solo or collaborative activity.

 The **Assessment** section offers questions to ask yourself when you are assessing students' understanding of the process and the content.

 In the **Differentiation** section, you will find two levels of differentiation. The first level scaffolds and adapts the task for students who struggle with reading independently and retaining information. The second level extends the activity and offers more challenge to students who can read independently and retain information.

 The **Variations** section offers two different activities, based on the lesson strategy, to enhance reading engagement. We all know that routine can benefit many students. Yet, sometimes changing things around can motivate them.

Connections to the Common Core State Standards

The lessons and activities in this book will help you meet the following Common Core State Standards (CCSS) for English Language Arts.

Lesson	RI.3.1	RI.3.2	RI.3.3	RI.3.4	RI.3.5	RI.3.7	RI.3.8	RI.3.9	RI.3.10	RI.4.1	RI.4.2	RI.4.3	RI.4.4	RI.4.5	RI.4.7	RI.4.8	RI.4.9	RI.4.10	RI.5.1	RI.5.2	RI.5.3	RI.5.4	RI.5.5	RI.5.7	RI.5.8	RI.5.9	RI.5.10
GRADE 3										**GRADE 4**									**GRADE 5**								
1	•								•	•								•	•								•
2	•								•	•								•	•								•
3		•							•		•							•		•							•
4			•						•			•						•			•						•
5	•								•	•								•	•								•
6	•								•	•								•	•								•
7		•							•		•							•		•							•
8	•								•	•								•	•								•
9		•							•		•							•		•							•
10		•							•		•							•		•							•
11		•							•		•							•		•							•
12					•				•					•				•					•				•
13					•				•					•				•					•				•
14					•				•					•				•					•				•
15					•				•					•				•					•				•
16					•				•					•				•					•				•
17					•				•					•				•					•				•
18				•					•				•					•				•					•
19				•					•				•					•				•					•
20				•					•				•					•				•					•
21					•				•					•				•					•				•
22					•				•					•				•					•				•
23						•			•						•			•							•		•
24							•		•							•		•						•			•
25						•			•							•		•								•	•
26							•		•								•	•						•			•
27								•	•								•	•								•	•
28								•	•								•	•								•	•
29								•	•								•	•								•	•
30									•								•	•								•	•

Lesson 1

Situated Stickies

 ## What Is It?

Inferring from text is a complicated skill that often requires guided practice. When using Situated Stickies, students write down inferences on sticky notes as they read and place them next to the relevant sentences in the text. The inferences are then shared in a group to ensure accuracy of understanding. By identifying text-based evidence that leads to particular inferences, students begin to understand texts on a deeper level. This interaction with text aids in the processing of information and retention of knowledge.

 ## Why Use It?

Inferring is a difficult, yet important, reading comprehension strategy. When proficient readers infer, they construct meaning from the text by searching for meaning that is not explicitly stated (Keene, 2008) or "right there" (Raphael and Au, 2006). When readers infer, they combine prior knowledge with what they read and make interpretations. It is important that interpretations are based on accurate information from both prior knowledge and correct understanding of the text. Students need to understand that there can be hidden meaning in a text. For example, if the text says, "During the Dust Bowl many people moved from their farms," students may infer that people lost their homes, moved away from friends and loved ones, had to depend on others, and so forth.

 ## Text Selection

The text used for Situated Stickies must lend itself to inferring and thinking beyond simple statements in a text. Almost any informational text would work, even the most straightforward example. At first glance, the following sentence seems quite literal:

The population of Nashville, Tennessee, is approximately 600,000.

The depth of inferential understanding will depend on students' prior knowledge. Compared to New York City, which has a population of over 8 million, Nashville is small. Yet, compared to a small town of 5,000 to 10,000 people, Nashville is huge. Other inferences could be the number of stores, jobs, diversity within the city, and so forth.

⟲ Instructional Steps

Introduction

1. Introduce students to the concept of inferences.

2. Say to students, "Most snakes live in tropical regions."

3. Explain that tropical regions are warm all year long and ask what this might imply. (Answers might include that warm weather makes it easier for snakes to live, there is more food in warmer climates, or snakes have more places to hide since there is greenery all year long.)

4. Continue in this manner with the following sentences:

   The Grand Canyon was carved by the Colorado River.

   Tornadoes can have wind speeds up to 300 miles per hour.

   Llamas are very social animals, but they sometimes spit at each other!

5. Introduce the selection that students are to read independently.

6. Hand out a specific number of sticky notes to students. The amount will depend on the length of the text and the number of inferences you would like them to make.

7. Explain that they will use the sticky notes as they read to help them "mark" sentences in the text that state a very important point about the topic.

8. Explain to students that they are to focus on finding areas in the text where they can make inferences.

Teacher Modeling and Guided Practice

1. Read the beginning of your selection with students or use the sample text provided.

2. Select a sentence that allows for inferring and ask students for the "broader" meaning of the sentence.

3. Discuss what they might write on a sticky note near that sentence.

4. Write the ideas on a chart or whiteboard and have students select one to put on the text near the selected sentence.

5. Repeat the process until students understand. When they are ready, they can work on their own.

6. Lead students to deeper understanding by asking them guiding questions. For example, if after reading the sentence "Scientists are concerned that sharks are becoming extinct," the student has written, "There may be no more sharks," he is showing some level of understanding. But if the student has written, "Sharks

Text

Giant panda bears live in the country of China. In China, the panda is called "Xiongmao," which means "large bear-cats." The giant panda has protected status in China. The Chinese consider this animal a national treasure.

Giant pandas live in the rainforest high in the mountains of western China. The main food for panda bears is bamboo, and they can spend up to 12 hours a day eating the bamboo!

Class Model

Giant pandas are protected in China because they are on the endangered species list. China cares about their animals like we do.

are becoming an endangered species," he has not only understood, but has categorized his learning. Guiding questions to extend thinking with the first response could be "What does that tell you about the animal?" or "What will that mean?"

Some other guiding questions might be:

What does this connect to?

Who or what else might this affect?

What word signals that there is more than what we are reading?

Who is writing this and why?

Is this a fact or an opinion?

What more do you need to know?

Directions for Independent Application

1. As students read, they select sentences that are "broader" than written. Tell students to stop at that point, write one or two inferences on a sticky note, and place it near the sentence from which they are drawing the inferences.

2. Students continue this process until all sticky notes have been used.

Taking Ownership

Divide students into groups of two or three and have them share the sentences that led them to an inference and explain how they arrived at their conclusions. Students write a summary page of their inferences as they identify the evidence that supports these inferences. The writing can be completed as a group or solo assignment.

Assessment

When assessing students' inferences, ask yourself the following.

✔ Does the information in the inference logically connect to the text?

✔ Is all the information correct?

✔ Does the work contain sufficient details?

Differentiation

✦ To scaffold this task, select the sentences you want students to focus on. Also, give students a list of leading questions.

✦ To extend this task, have students choose two or three of their selected sentences and rewrite them with the inference included.

Variations

✦ Use Situated Stickies to summarize information. Students write down main ideas and supporting facts. Then in pairs or triads, they use the information from the sticky notes to summarize the text.

✦ Use Situated Stickies to help students identify unfamiliar vocabulary. As students read, they search for unknown words in the text that they can define by using context clues. Students write what they think the word means on a sticky note. Partners then discuss the meaning of the unknown words.

Wrap It

What Is It?

This activity allows students to engage in learning by using a rap song to aid in the retention of information. As students read, they write down approximately three to four main point phrases from the text. Then, working in small groups, students put these phrases together coherently to create a rap song. Show students how to string together phrases into coherent, full-meaning sections. Once students have written the rap song, they should share it with the class, another class, or anyone else who will listen because each repetition helps them to retain the information—that is, "wrap up" the knowledge.

Why Use It?

The ability to pull key phrases from a text and combine them while retaining the original meaning is the beginning of learning how to summarize. Summarizing aids students in their organization of text information and in analyzing the extracted information so that it can be critiqued for understanding and communication (Gomez, Herman, and Gomez, 2007). Summarizing gives students an opportunity to communicate important information from a text and monitor their own understanding. Summarizing also allows teachers to assess students' ability to capture the main points from a text, which is a critical component in assuring that readers are constructing meaning from the text. In addition, Fink's (2011) work on using rap in the classroom has shown that it fosters excitement, motivation, and higher levels of reading proficiency.

Text Selection

Most informational texts will work with this strategy. A compare and contrast text structure would allow for interesting content.

⟳ Instructional Steps

Introduction

1. Explain to students that they will be selecting and writing down key phrases from the text as they read. They will be looking for parts of sentences that convey important facts about the subject of the text.

2. Make it clear that the phrase may be taken complete from the sentence or paraphrased as long as it retains the same meaning.

3. Tell students they will be using these phrases to write a rap song.

Teacher Modeling and Guided Practice

1. Write the following sentences on the board to model how phrases can be selected.

   "Jupiter is the biggest planet in our universe. Its surface is surrounded by yellow and red clouds."

2. Read the sentences and underline phrases that would be important for students to know about Jupiter: *biggest planet, surrounded by yellow and red clouds.*

3. Make sure students understand that you have selected parts of the sentences that relay important information about Jupiter.

Strategy *in Action*

Text

An anemometer is what weather scientists use to measure the speed of the wind. The wind makes little cup-like features on the anemometer spin around. The wind speed can be determined by how fast the anemometer is spinning.

Class Model

(Sing to a rap beat)

ANEMOMETERS

Anemometers are what we need

Measuring wind, measuring speed

Fast or slow—the wind can go

Anemometers

Like odometers

Measure speed—yes, indeed!

Fast or slow—wind makes them go!

4. As a class put these phrases together in a rap song. Explain that singing the rap song will help jog their memory about Jupiter.

5. Perform the rap song together as a class.

Directions for Independent Application

1. Assign intended text.

2. Have students read and write down short phrases that contain important information about the topic.

3. Let students work in small groups and use the selected phrases to write a rap song.

 Taking Ownership

In small groups, students share the selected phrases, agree the information is stated correctly, and write a rap song to "wrap up" the knowledge. Students then share the rap song with the class.

 Assessment

When assessing the students' rap songs, ask yourself the following:

✔ Is the information accurate?

✔ Did the information keep its integrity as the students changed the sentence structure and trimmed the information to fit into phrases?

✔ Do the topics flow in an informational and identifiable manner?

✔ Does the overall rap song make sense?

 Differentiation

✦ To scaffold this task, aid students in the selection of their first and second phrases and explain why these phrases are important.

✦ To extend this task, have students choose the important phrases and rewrite them in their own words. Be specific; tell students they may retain only 50 percent of the original phrase.

 Variations

✦ Students use selected phrases to write a type of song of their choosing.

✦ Students use the phrases to write a freestyle poem. You can find multiple examples of poems containing expository information in books and on the Web.

Lesson 3

Blogging

 ## What Is It?

In this activity, students write a blog entry based on what they have read. They read a passage and write down important facts, then use the facts to write a paragraph about the topic. The writing should be interesting and accurate, as it will be posted on a class blog for a worldwide audience. On the blog, students invite questions or comments about the topic, making it an interactive site. Prior to this activity, you must create a blog for the class. Search the Internet for "How to create a blog" to bring up multiple sites with easy-to-follow directions.

 ## Why Use It?

One of the best motivators for writers of any age is knowing that their writing will be shared with others for a purpose. When a writer publishes material, the stakes are higher for accuracy in all areas of writing, including content, coherence, voice, and mechanics. In the classroom, blogs can be a valuable tool for teaching communication skills and allowing students to reach out internationally (Carmelina Films, "Blogging in the Classroom," 2009). The blog gives students a worldwide audience. It has been shown that the role of audience, when considering new media-infused learning environments, impacts the writing and motivation (Magnifico, 2010). Using blogs in the classroom teaches students the importance of accuracy and communication for both the writer and the audience of this relatively new type of journalism.

 ## Text Selection

Any informational text can be used for this blogging activity.

 ## Instructional Steps

Introduction

1. Ask students how many of them have read a blog. If students seem uncertain, explain that a blog is on the Internet and is a series of short writing pieces on a topic.

Strategy *in Action*

Text

Tigers are the largest cats in the world. They are meat eaters. Tigers are orange and have black stripes. Adult tigers can weigh over 700 pounds and grow to 11 feet long. A grown tiger's tail is about three feet long.

Class Model

Julie / January 6
Mrs. Witherell's Blog

TIGERS

Tigers are fascinating animals. They are the biggest cats on earth. A tiger eats meat and that might be why some tigers weigh over 700 pounds. Tigers can grow to be 11 feet long, which is longer than a couch.

2. Show a blog as a model. Select a sample blog on the same topic you will be exploring.

3. Say to students, "When writing entries for a blog, the most recent entry is placed on top." Explain that the class is going to make a blog, and students will be posting their writing for the entire world to see.

Teacher Modeling and Guided Practice

1. Show additional model blog sites. Searching "blogs for children" or "elementary class blogs" will bring up a number of sites, although you must choose with care. Discuss the organization of the model blog and your expectations for the writing of the students' blog pieces.

2. Using a short text, model and have students help you select two to three important facts from the text.

3. Together, write a summary that would be blog-worthy.

Directions for Independent Application

1. Students write down three to four important facts from the assigned text as they read.

2. Make students responsible for accurate information. Students work in pairs and show their partner where in the text they found the information.

3. The partner should verify with his or her initials that the information is accurate.

4. Each student writes a blog entry in paragraph form, in the style and format that you prefer (e.g., student name, date, title, text). Students edit their pieces and share their final drafts with the group.

5. Help students post their pieces on the blog. Students should decide the order of the blog entries and upload them accordingly.

Taking Ownership

Students can periodically check the blog and answer questions or comments that refer to the summary information in their blog post.

Assessment

When assessing the students' blog entries, ask yourself the following:

✔ Is all the information correct?

✔ Are the key ideas supported by facts?

✔ Does the summary reflect the text read?

✔ Is the piece formatted as you requested?

If the blogs will be posted online, be sure that the pieces are publication-worthy. Carefully consider the order of the pieces as you post them, so as to create a logical structure for the blog.

Differentiation

✦ To scaffold this activity, have students choose two important facts to write about. Then have them create a graphic to be added to the blog.

✦ To extend this task, have students go beyond the assigned text and research more information and include four to six facts (at least two that are not in the assigned text). If possible, have them find a public domain picture to add to the blog.

Variations

✦ Instead of writing paragraphs, have students write their facts in a letter to you that will be posted on the blog. Be sure they use proper letter format.

✦ Instead of writing paragraphs, students create slideshow presentations to post on the blog. They may choose one important fact per slide, or each student may create his or her own slide.

RI.3.3 · RI.4.3 · RI.5.3

Possible Sentences Plus

 ## What Is It?

Students synthesize information to make a new true statement. As students read, they write down facts. They use these facts to write a sentence or two by putting at least two facts or domain-specific words together to make a possible (true) sentence, for example, "Jupiter is the fifth planet and is surrounded by clouds." Students will then also write an impossible (false) sentence using one fact and one false statement, for example, "Earth is the third planet from the sun and has two moons." At the end of each statement students identify whether the statement is possible or impossible.

 ## Why Use It?

Possible Sentences Plus is an interactive strategy that encourages students to think about and to begin to synthesize information. Synthesis, as a category within Bloom's Taxonomy, is considered a "higher order" thinking skill. When students synthesize, they say information differently by combining information from two or more sources, such as text, media, primary sources, or background knowledge. At the basic level, information comes from two or more sentences; at the broader level, information comes from two or more sources. By synthesizing, students show an understanding of the big ideas and concepts in informational texts (Block and Duffy, 2008). As they begin to learn to synthesize, students often "chunk" information together. According to Cummins and Stallmeyer-Gerard (2011) students who engage in synthesizing move from just stating facts to compiling information into the big ideas or major concepts. Possible Sentences Plus introduces the synthesizing skill by having students chunk information, but also think about the big ideas and concepts by writing and recognizing both possible and impossible sentences.

 ## Text Selection

Choose a text that corresponds to the skills you are trying to foster with your students. If you are working on compare and contrast skills, the possible sentences could be built around the compare and contrast text structure. In order to make this activity the most effective, the text should contain more than just simple facts.

Instructional Steps

Introduction

1. Explain to students that as they read they will write down at least four important facts from the text.

2. Say to students, "After you finish reading, you are going to use these facts to make possible sentences. You will need to make sure your facts are accurate."

3. Tell students they will use the facts to write two possible statements and one foil, or false, statement that they will use in a group game.

Teacher Modeling and Guided Practice

1. Model the activity for students by using the following four facts about Idaho's geography. Write the facts on the board, and then discuss two possible sentences.

> Idaho is a Rocky Mountain state.
>
> Northern Idaho has lots of forests.
>
> Southern Idaho has desert land.
>
> Central Idaho has the landmark Craters of the Moon.

Strategy *in Action*

Text

The southern state of Mississippi was first discovered by Hernando de Sota in the mid 1500s. The capital of Mississippi is Jackson. The state flower is the magnolia. Southern Mississippi borders the ocean. In Mississippi cotton, corn, peanuts, sugar cane, rice, and pecans are grown. Petroleum is also produced.

Class Model

Possible Sentence: Mississippi is a southern state and is on the ocean.

Possible Sentence: Mississippi produces cotton and petroleum.

Impossible Sentence: New Orleans and Jackson are the two largest cities in Mississippi.

Two possible sentences could be:

Idaho has forests and deserts.

Idaho has a famous landmark and is in the Rocky Mountains.

2. Discuss the possible sentences with students and explain that for fun you are going to make an impossible sentence. Share the following two sentences and ask which one is impossible:

There are forests in the mountains of Idaho.

The ocean meets the desert in Idaho.

Directions for Independent Application

1. Students read the assigned text and write down four facts from the passage.

2. Next, they put two of the facts together to make a possible, or true, sentence.

3. They then use at least one fact and either another fact in an incorrect manner or something made up to create an impossible, or false, sentence.

4. Students write the three sentences to share. They label each sentence as possible or impossible.

 ## Taking Ownership

In a game-like fashion, small groups take turns reading their sentences, trying to bluff when reading the impossible sentence. The rest of the class guesses which sentences are possible and which is impossible.

 ## Assessment

When assessing students' possible and impossible sentences, ask yourself the following:

✔ Do the possible sentences have correct information and are they synthesized to retain the correct meaning?

✔ For the possible sentences, is the information based on what is included in the text?

✔ Is there a connection or relationship between the two facts in the possible sentences?

✔ Is the impossible sentence false?

Additionally, to assess where your students are in their cognitive abilities, analyze the possible sentences to see if students are simply connecting two facts or if the broader concept is evident.

Differentiation

✦ To scaffold this task, have students write a possible sentence using just one fact. They may also use only one "fact" to write the impossible sentence.

✦ To extend this task, have students write a paragraph that includes an impossible statement. They then exchange papers and identify the false statement within the written paragraph.

 ## Variations

✦ In a "Believe It or Not" game, students write three sentences that are true or three sentences that are false about the topic. They read the sentences to a group and the group decides to "Believe It or Not."

✦ Instead of possible or impossible statements, students write two possible and one statement that contains an altered fact from the text, such as "Idaho has 30 million people." The other students identify the misinformation and correct it by stating, "Idaho has about 2 million people."

RI.3.1 RI.4.1 RI.5.1

Highlighting

What Is It?

Students identify *important* versus *interesting* information in a text. Students use either highlighter markers or tape to select and highlight important words and key statements. Allow only so much highlighter tape to be used, or give a limited number of inches of highlighter ink in the complete passage. This will force students to limit their selections to the most important information and resist the urge to include interesting details.

Why Use It?

Highlighting text is a rite of passage, but it's often done mindlessly. How many of us have given a student a highlighter only to find the end result is a page that is more yellow than white? When students do this, they are telling us something—that they need help in identifying important information. Teaching students to highlight important facts and ideas helps them to glean from the text the pieces they need to learn and remember. It's important to emphasize the concept of *important* versus *interesting*. According to Keene (2008), determining importance in text can be approached at three levels: word level, where main words carry meaning; sentence level, in which key sentences portray main concepts; and finally, text level, where key information from the complete text is considered. When highlighting, we teach students to work at the word and sentence levels. Eventually, as students become more familiar with this skill, they will develop a greater sense of understanding at the text level.

Text Selection

This activity will work with virtually any content or topic. However, it is best initially to use text in which the important points are easy to distinguish from interesting information. In addition, consider the size of the print. Be sure that it is large enough to accommodate the highlighting—using print that is 14 to 16 points is helpful.

Instructional Steps

Introduction

1. Explain to students that highlighting is a great strategy to help them mark what is important in a text. Point out that they need to be careful how much of the information they select to highlight to avoid highlighting most of the page.

2. Tell students that before they highlight, they have to determine whether a word, phrase, or sentence is important enough to be highlighted.

3. Read aloud the following sentence:

   "The blue whale is the largest whale and can be as long as three school buses put together."

   Explain to students that the *important* information is that the blue whale is the largest whale, but it is *interesting* that it can be as long as three school buses. So, they would only need to highlight the first part of the sentence.

4. Ask students to identify the important points and the interesting details in this sentence:

   "Mumps is an infection that causes the saliva glands to swell between the jaw and the ear, making people look like they have chipmunk cheeks."

   Students should be able to identify that (1) mumps is an infection and (2) saliva glands swell are important points. People looking like they have chipmunk cheeks is an interesting detail.

5. Mention that it is sufficient to highlight "Mumps is an infection" and "saliva glands swell."

Teacher Modeling and Guided Practice

1. Using the sample text, show students how thoughtful highlighting is done as you talk them through the process. Display it on an overhead projector or an interactive board that allows you to highlight.

2. Repeat the process using at least three paragraphs of an informational text.

3. In the first and second paragraph of your passage, select and highlight important information. Explain why you feel these words, phrases, or sentences convey key information from the text.

4. For the third paragraph, have students discuss with partners what they think should be highlighted. Then, have them share and explain why they have chosen these words, phrases, or sentences to represent key ideas from the text.

Strategy *in Action*

Text

Quartz is a very common mineral. It is made of silica and oxygen. There are different kinds of quartz, some have large crystals, while others have small ones. Citrine and amethyst are types of quartz. Quartz can be found in geodes. A geode, which is the official state rock of Iowa, looks like a regular rock, but when cracked open has quartz or crystals inside.

Class Model–Highlighted Text

Quartz is a very common mineral. It is made of silica and oxygen. There are different kinds of quartz, some have large crystals, while others have small ones. Citrine and amethyst are types of quartz. Quartz can be found in geodes. A geode, which is the official state rock of Iowa, looks like a regular rock, but when cracked open has quartz or crystals inside.

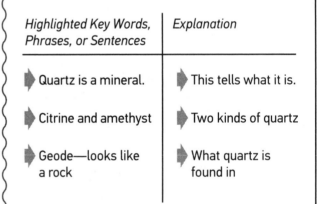

Highlighted Key Words, Phrases, or Sentences	Explanation
Quartz is a mineral.	This tells what it is.
Citrine and amethyst	Two kinds of quartz
Geode—looks like a rock	What quartz is found in

Quartz is a rock-like mineral that is found in geodes.

Directions for Independent Application

1. Assign students a text and give them highlighters or highlighter tape.

2. Students highlight the text as they read. Remind them that they need to carefully choose the key ideas—words, phrases, and sentences—that they want to mark in the text with their highlighter or tape. Limit the amount that can be highlighted.

3. Students create a T-chart to record what they highlighted and explain each choice. They should also include a summary sentence under the chart.

Taking Ownership

Students write down three key words, phrases, or sentences they have chosen to highlight. They explain their choices either in writing or to a partner. Then they write a summary sentence of the passage.

 ## Assessment

When assessing the students' highlighted pieces, ask yourself the following:

✔ Did the student select important words, phrases, and text?

✔ Does the "whole" represent the main idea of the text?

✔ Do the student's explanations for highlighting these pieces make sense?

✔ Does the summary sentence reflect the key points?

 ## Differentiation

✦ To scaffold this task, limit the highlighting. If you are working with highlighting tape, give students three pieces, one short and two long. Tell students to select one important word and two key sentences or sentence parts.

✦ To extend this task, have students highlight for a specific text structure, such as parts that show cause and effect, parts that show chronological order, or parts of the text that show contrast.

 ## Variations

✦ Using a magnifying glass (or facsimile cutout) students focus on important parts in the text. Next, they write down the key words or sentences they observed.

✦ Make a copy of the text and have students cut out the key words and key sentences. Give students an index card or half of an index card depending on the size of the original text. Students should glue the key words and ideas onto the card. This physical space will limit what a student chooses as important.

Text Messaging

What Is It?

Students write text messages to a friend on a cell phone graphic organizer. The messages must include important, abbreviated facts from the informational reading. The writing, in the form of a text message, uses phrase structure rather than full sentences. In essence, as students read, they "text message" important facts from the material. One of the text messages must use a picture (image) format.

Why Use It?

Sometimes we just need to know the facts. When teaching students to separate *important* from *interesting*, teachers often have students highlight text with highlighters or highlighter tape. Text messages work in a similar way. We use abbreviations and write exactly to the point. When students need to know information, sometimes the "shorthand" facts are enough. While focusing on facts helps a reader understand the gist of a text, picking out key details deepens comprehension. But details are sometimes easy to miss. All of us miss some details when we are reading (Fisher, Lapp, and Wood, 2011). Effective reading requires a reader to obtain information from the text and make his or her own meaning (Grabe and Stoller, 2001). Helping students identify important facts and key details influences the meaning they construct. Because text messages are short communications, they are a good tool to help students focus on details and facts, and thus reinforce their understanding of what they read.

Text Selection

A text written in a description text structure would be best for this activity. Since, by nature, a text message is simple, a straightforward text or section of a text should be used for this activity.

Instructional Steps

Introduction

1. Ask students how many of them have received or sent text messages. Discuss the differences between a text message, an email, and a letter.

2. Ask students if they (or their parent/guardian) have received or sent image texts—messages that contain pictures.

3. Tell students that they are going to "text message" important details and facts from their reading to other students in the room. They will also be sending one "image" text.

Teacher Modeling and Guided Practice

1. Read an informational paragraph and discuss how to translate important facts and details into a "text message," then write the message on the board. For instance, in reading about elephants, you might text: "elephants r mammals" or "2 main types of elephants, African & Asian," or "elephants r largest land animals."

2. Have students give you a few "text messages" of their own from the paragraph.

3. Stress that as you write the "text messages," you are reading for key details and want to pull out just the important information.

4. Discuss possible "image" text messages that could be sent on this topic.

Strategy *in Action*

Text

Did you know there is a long word to describe rain, snow, hail, and sleet? The word is *precipitation*. Precipitation occurs when water is released from the atmosphere to the earth's surface. The water can be liquid, like rain, or it can be solid, like snow.

Class Model

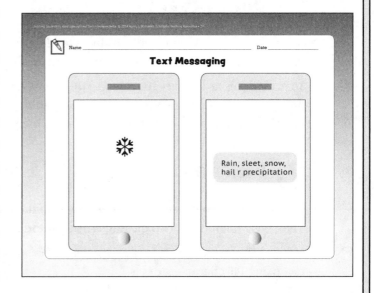

Directions for Independent Application

1. Distribute copies of the Text Messaging graphic organizer.

2. Students read the assigned passage and write a "text message" on the graphic organizer.

3. Remind them that the "text message" must contain important facts or details about the topic.

4. Make it clear that one "text message" must be an image.

 ## Taking Ownership

In pairs, students exchange text messages and reply to each other in another text message. Students should include important details in their replies. Then students put the text messages in chronological order so they make sense when being read, and resemble a texted conversation about the content.

 ## Assessment

When assessing the students' text messaging entries, ask yourself the following:

✔ Is all the information in the text messages correct?

✔ Do the text messages demonstrate understanding of the material?

✔ Do the text messages give any examples from the text?

✔ Are inferences supported?

 ## Differentiation

✦ To scaffold this task, work with students to identify important facts and details in the text. Have them paraphrase these details into text messages.

✦ To extend this task, have students use the "conversation" mode and create a text message conversation of their own on the graphic organizer, with messages being "sent" back and forth. Have this conversation include short quotes.

 ## Variations

✦ Give students two new domain-specific vocabulary words that relate to the text. Then have them "text" two messages using these words.

✦ Instead of a text message, further challenge the students by having them "tweet" a fact using 140 characters or less.

Name _____

Date _____

Text Messaging

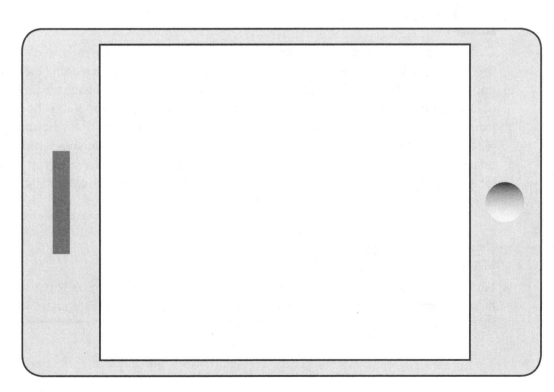

Double-Column Note Taking

MEETING THE COMMON CORE
RI.3.2   RI.4.2   RI.5.2

 ## What Is It?

Students are taught an adaptation of the two-column (T-chart) method of Cornell note-taking. The Cornell method of note-taking instructs readers to divide their paper into two columns. Students write important facts and ideas from a text on the right side of their paper. After writing the notes on the right side, they then write a short summary phrase on the left. This note-taking technique can be used with both books and lectures. To study, students can fold back the right side and show only the summary. They then quiz themselves by looking at the summary words or phrases and trying to recall the details on the right side. If they cannot remember, they can check their notes and try again.

 ## Why Use It?

Children in elementary school are not usually assigned to "take notes," but we do expect them to remember facts. Research shows that combining writing with reading increases both reading comprehension and knowledge retention. Taking notes while reading organizes thoughts and promotes reading comprehension by fostering connections from one idea to the next (Graham and Hebert, 2010). When students state the main idea as they summarize, they are categorizing. This helps readers understand the relationship of different concepts. Taking notes has been shown to aid readers by facilitating understanding and allowing students to return to the information and retrieve the knowledge (Rahmani and Sadeghi, 2011).

 ## Text Selection

For students who are beginning to learn how to use this method, choose a text with bold headings that clearly state key concepts. Students can rely on these headings to support them in writing the summary phrase on the left.

Strategy *in Action*

Text

Endangered species are animals that are in danger of becoming extinct. Extinct means that these animals no longer exist. All classes of animals have endangered species—both vertebrates, such as birds, fish, mammals, reptiles, and amphibians, and also invertebrates, like clams. One of the main reasons animals become endangered is because they lose their habitat. This is often caused by weather or construction. Sometimes exotic species, which are new to the area, arrive and cause problems for native plants and hinder plant growth. Sometimes animals, such as whales, are over-hunted. Since too many whales were caught, the population began dying out. Sometimes animals become endangered because of natural causes, like disease, or unnatural causes, like pollution.

Class Model

Summary	Facts From the Text
Endangered	Animals could become extinct
All classes of animals have endangered species	Vertebrates and invertebrates
Why animals become endangered	Habitat destruction—weather, construction Exotic species—new to area and cause problems for the native plants and hinder plant growth Over-hunted—like whales, too many were caught and the population was dying out Natural and unnatural causes—disease, pollution

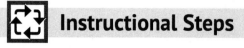 **Instructional Steps**

Introduction

1. Explain to students that they are going to try a new kind of note-taking when they read their book or article.

2. Using a plain piece of writing paper, show students how to fold the paper vertically so there is a fold line about one-third from the left side of the paper.

3. Unfold the paper and draw a line on the fold line. Explain that this chart will help students organize their notes. Set up a similar two-column note organizer on the board so students can see your work.

Teacher Modeling and Guided Practice

1. Read a short text with students and show on the board how to write notes in the right column.

2. As you read, select important information containing facts, ideas, and supporting details. Discuss how the details support the facts or ideas as you write.

3. After the first detail or two, look at your notes and decide on a summary heading or phrase to write on the left side. Repeat this step until students are comfortable.

4. Have students help you with the procedure for the final part of the text.

5. Fold the paper back or cover the notes column so everyone can only see the summary column. Together, try to remember the details on the fact side.

Directions for Independent Application

1. Students fold their papers and make the two-column line.

2. Students write notes in the right column as they read. Remind them to create summary headings in the left column.

3. After they are done, students work together to check their memory by folding the right column back to view just the summary column and seeing how many of the details they actually remember from the reading and note-taking.

Taking Ownership

Working individually, students fold the paper so they can see only the summary column. They try to recall the details that came from within the text, checking themselves by referring to their notes in the right column. If the student does not recall the details correctly, he or she goes back to the text and rereads the section that contains the missed information.

Assessment

When assessing the students' work, ask yourself the following:

✔ Is all the information on the note-taking sheet correct?

✔ Does the summary heading on the left reflect the facts and ideas on the right?

✔ Do the notes contain details that support the facts or ideas given?

Differentiation

✦ To scaffold this task, select three main areas of the text that encompass the most pertinent information. Have students take notes on these three areas.

✦ To extend this activity, have students add a third column to the chart. The first column is for notes, the second column is for the summary/main points, and the third column is for the student to write an opinion or connection about the information.

Variations

✦ Students "Take Note and Draw," in which the paper is divided into two columns, one for notes, the other to draw a picture or graphic of what the notes represent.

✦ With "Sticky-Note Notes," students write each fact on a sticky note. They then group the sticky notes, place each group on a sheet of paper, and title each page with the main idea. Students will need multiple pieces of paper.

Wish Upon a Star

 What Is It?

This activity allows students to organize facts and information from a text. Using a star graphic organizer, students put the title or topic of the book, chapter, or section in the middle of the star. They then write five important facts—one in each of the points of the star. Under the star, on the lines provided, students write what they learned from the text, an opinion about what they learned, and a "wish," which is a question that asks something else they would like to know about the topic.

 Why Use It?

"Wish Upon a Star" is primarily a motivator for students to write a question about the information they are reading. Questioning gives students a new perspective when interacting with text. Questioning allows readers to be in an active and purposeful role as they learn from the text (Taboada and Guthrie, 2006). For English Language Learners (ELLs), questioning has multiple advantages for concept development and increased reading comprehension in the content areas (Taboada, Bianco, and Bowerman, 2012). Forming a question requires understanding and thinking about a text. The questions students ask provide a window into their comprehension of the material they read.

 Text Selection

Any general informational text would work with this activity. It is best to avoid a text with the question-and-answer text structure because it could inhibit students formulating their own questions.

 Instructional Steps

Introduction

1. Explain to students that they are going to be taking notes on a star graphic organizer as they read.

2. Say, "Since the star has only five points, you must select your facts carefully because only the most important information is written down."

Teacher Modeling and Guided Practice

1. Display an enlarged version of the Wish Upon a Star graphic organizer.

2. Use a short informational text and write the topic in the middle of the star.

3. Pick out the first two pieces of information and explain to students why you have chosen these facts for the points of the star.

4. Have students help you select the information for the remaining three points of the star.

5. After writing the notes, discuss a main idea, an opinion about the text, and a wish. The wish is a question that asks something else you want to know about the topic.

Strategy *in Action*

Text

The rainforest covers six percent of the earth's surface and is important in making oxygen for the earth. We must breathe oxygen to live. The rainforest is hot and humid as the temperature is high and there is lots of moisture. There are four layers of the rainforest: the emergent, canopy, understory, and forest. The largest rainforest in the world is the Amazon Rainforest in South America. It is almost the size of the mainland United States and covers about 40 percent of South America.

Class Model

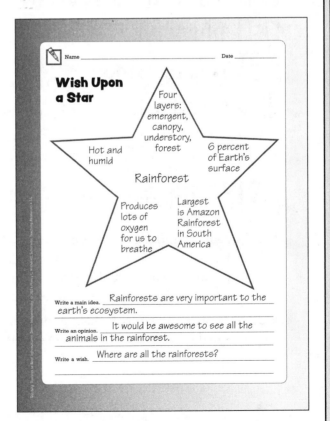

Directions for Independent Application

1. Distribute copies of the Wish Upon a Star graphic organizer.

2. Students use the graphic organizer, filling out the center and the points as they read.

3. Students write a main idea, an opinion, and a wish on the lines below the star after they have finished reading.

 ## Taking Ownership

Students work with a small group and discuss their main ideas, opinions, and wishes.

 ## Assessment

When assessing the students' Wish Upon a Star graphic organizer, ask yourself the following:

✔ Are all the facts on the star correct?

✔ Is the main idea statement correct?

✔ Does the opinion reflect any inferences from the reading?

✔ Is the wish (question) based on topic information?

 ## Differentiation

✦ To scaffold this task, discuss the main idea/topic with students prior to their reading.

✦ To extend this task, have students refer to the text and write a sentence that defends their opinion.

 ## Variations

✦ After reading the selected passage, students "Make a Wish" by writing one question related to the text on a star. The answer to the question must come from the text. Depending on the number of students in the group, pick a few "wishes" to read aloud to the class for other students to answer.

✦ Use the graphic organizer to make a summary star. Students put five facts on the outside of the star near each point, then write a short summary inside the star.

Name _____ Date _____

Wish Upon a Star

Write a main idea. _____

_____

Write an opinion. _____

_____

Write a wish. _____

_____

Mnemonics

What Is It?

A mnemonic device is used to help us trigger our memory about certain events or pieces of information. When teaching my third graders, for example, we classify vertebrates through the mnemonic device FARM B, which stands for fish, amphibians, reptiles, mammals, and birds. This mnemonic device helps the students (and me) remember the five classes of vertebrates. In this lesson, students read a text and list the important facts, including any domain-specific vocabulary, then create their own mnemonic device.

Why Use It?

The mnemonic device is a well-recognized strategy to help us recall information. Whether we use "Roy G. Biv" to recall the colors of the rainbow (red, orange, yellow, green, blue, indigo, violet) or the sentence "Every good boy does fine" to remember the lines on the music scale (egbdf), mnemonic devices offer us instant recall. The device aids us in retaining information and triggers the recall. Studies have shown that mnemonic devices can also aid students with learning disabilities in their recall of important information (Scruggs, Mastropieri, Berkeley, and Marshak, 2010). A mnemonic device should be based on relatable information that helps the brain make a connection. According to Amiryousefi and Ketabi (2011) a mnemonic is a memory enhancing instructional strategy that involves teaching students to link new information to known information. The authors also suggest when learners create their own mnemonic devices, they will be more apt to remember the information.

Text Selection

A text that offers a short list to memorize is a good choice for students learning to create mnemonics. For example, the text in the last lesson stated that the rainforest has four layers: emergent, canopy, understory, and forest. This type of information can be easily made into a mnemonic— "Ed Can Use Food."

Instructional Steps

Introduction

1. Explain to students that a mnemonic device is used to help us remember information.

2. Share some mnemonic devices with the class. Some ideas: HOMES for the five great lakes (Huron, Ontario, Michigan, Erie, and Superior); "Mary visits every Monday, just staying until noon" represents planets in their spacial order.

3. Tell students they are going to learn how to make their own mnemonic devices.

Teacher Modeling and Guided Practice

1. Read a short text with important information and model how you would pick out the information you want to retain. For instance, when reading a text on the three main types of trees—deciduous, evergreen, and coniferous—the mnemonic "David eats corn" could be used.

2. Read another article and have students help select the important information. Together, create a couple of mnemonic devices. Stress that the mnemonic device needs to be easy to remember.

Strategy *in Action*

Text

The United States government has three branches. Our forefathers made the three branches so we would have fair and strong government. The Legislative branch makes the laws. The Executive branch includes the President and carries out the laws. The Judicial branch oversees the court system and makes sure that the laws are being carried out.

Class Model

Mnemonic examples for the three branches of government: legislative, executive, and judicial:

• Let's eat jelly.

• LEJ

• Lobsters enjoy jokes.

Directions for Independent Application

1. Using the assigned text, students write down important information as they read.

2. Students create their own mnemonic device to remember the information they selected.

 Taking Ownership

Students share their mnemonic devices in groups. Each group then decides which mnemonic device is easiest to remember and shares it with the class.

 Assessment

When assessing students' mnemonic devices, ask yourself the following:

✔ Is all the information correct?

✔ Is there a clear link between the mnemonic device and the information that needs to be remembered?

✔ Does the mnemonic device appear easy to remember?

 Differentiation

◆ To scaffold this task, give students the words to the mnemonic device and have them write the facts that the words aid them in remembering.

◆ To extend this task, have students write a mnemonic device for something that must be remembered in order, such as the steps for completing long division.

 Variations

◆ Students create a mnemonic device by writing a song. The song can be set to a familiar tune such as "The Farmer in the Dell" or "Twinkle, Twinkle, Little Star."

◆ Students create a visual mnemonic. They draw a picture of each fact and put an association word with each picture.

MEETING THE COMMON CORE

RI.3.2 RI.4.2 RI.5.2

Lesson 10

Using Your Head(ings)

 ## What Is It?

Students use the headings of a text to organize an outline of the text's information. Headings automatically categorize information. As students read the text, they write down headings and list the main facts and important details from the corresponding sections of the text. The result is an outline with the topics and facts written clearly and in a way that information can be easily found.

 ## Why Use It?

Using the bold print to categorize book notes scaffolds students in their organization of written notes. The activity allows students to interact with the text in a very systematic way. The tactile movement employed as the student writes down information aids in storing the information for later retrieval. Note-taking, in any form, helps readers remember what was in a text. Headings—whether chapter titles or subheadings— play an important role in organizing information. According to Bluestein (2010), text features, such as bold headings, offer clues about what to focus on as we read, and as students view headings, they can more easily find the most important pieces of information within the body of the text. Learning to take good notes will help students when they need to refer back to their notes to support discussions or find answers with evidence from the text. Furthermore, learning to paraphrase is an important skill for writing papers that include text evidence, without plagiarizing.

 ## Text Selection

For this activity, choose a text with bold headings. Because the headings guide students' note-taking, starting with a text that has a large number of bold headings will make this activity easier.

Instructional Steps

Introduction

1. Point out to students the relevant bold print in the text and explain that these words are headings and that headings give us cues as to what the author is writing about. We can use these cues to organize notes.

2. Explain that note-taking is a technique that helps us remember information. Sometimes we may take notes from books, sometimes we may write notes when listening to someone speak. We write down the information that we want to refer to or quote at a later time.

3. Tell students that they will take notes about important facts as they read.

Teacher Modeling and Guided Practice

1. Using one section of a book similar to what they will be reading, show students different text features, such as bold words, italicized words, and captions.

2. Emphasize bold or italicized text as that which the author has identified as important information.

3. Point out a bold heading and explain that this tells the topic or subject of the section of the text to follow.

Strategy *in Action*

Text

CLOUDS

Clouds Are Water

Clouds are a large collection of very tiny droplets of water and sometimes ice crystals. They are so tiny and light that they can actually float in the air. Clouds are white because they reflect the light from the sun. When clouds get heavy because of all the tiny droplets of water or ice crystals, they turn a gray color.

Class Model

Clouds Are Water

Made of tiny droplets of water or tiny ice crystals

Droplets are so light they can float

Clouds reflect sunlight so are white

Gray clouds are heavy with the water droplets and ice crystals

4. Write the bold heading on chart paper to model taking notes.

5. Read the section with students and have them help you decide what information is important.

6. As you identify important information, paraphrase the language and write it down on the chart. Put each piece of information on its own line, indented under the bold heading line.

7. Model again with another bold-headed section of the text as you guide students to give you the correct information to write down.

Directions for Independent Application

1. Instruct students to use the headings for note-taking on their own or with a partner.

2. Students take notes as they read the assigned text.

3. As they begin, check to see that students understand the process.

 Taking Ownership

Students return to the headings and make them into questions. For example, the heading "The Lincoln Memorial" becomes "What is the Lincoln Memorial?" Students then try to see if they can answer the question using the details they have written beneath the heading. If not, they need to go back to the text and write down the missing information that would help them answer their question, or they need to reread the text for clarification.

 Assessment

When assessing students' note taking, ask yourself the following:

✔ Are all the bold headings included?

✔ Is all the information correct and under the right heading?

✔ Did the student paraphrase the information from the text?

Differentiation

✦ To scaffold this task, give students a paper with the bold headings already written on the paper. Go through one or two of the sections and work with students to choose the important information.

✦ To extend this task, after students have made the outline notes, let them choose one section, and use their notes to write a paragraph that includes all the important information.

 Variations

✦ Use index cards for the note-taking. Each bold-headed section goes on one index card. These can later be used as study cards.

✦ To make the topic division clearer, use two different colored pencils. Students write the bold heading in one color. Underneath the heading they write the notes in the other color.

Acrostic Fact Poem

 ## What Is It?

An acrostic fact poem is a poem that uses the letters in a word to write facts about a related topic. For instance, an acrostic fact poem on plants may look like this:

Photosynthesis
Living
Air
Nutrients
Traveling seeds
Stomata

Students read a text on the selected topic. They choose a word to represent that topic, for instance, polar bear may be represented by the word *polar* or *bear*. Students then write an acrostic poem that includes important facts from the text.

 ## Why Use It?

Writing an acrostic fact poem is an engaging and motivating method that gets students to look for important details in a text and apply knowledge to show understanding. Acrostic poems are easy to write because they don't need to rhyme, do not have to be full sentences, can be about any subject, and the lines can vary in length. As Ruurs (2011) states, "Acrostics are fun because they are word puzzles that can make poetry writing an exciting activity and encourage students to create their own poems" (page 38). An acrostic poem can be used as a mnemonic device to aid students in remembering important facts about a topic. Using acrostic fact poetry in content-area reading gives students a creative way to engage with important information from the text.

 ## Text Selection

A simple informational text with multiple facts about a topic can be used with this strategy. If the class needs more support, using a text with bold headings would help them choose important information.

Strategy *in Action*

Text

HUMPBACK WHALE

Humpback whales are large mammals that live in the ocean. They get their name from the dorsal fin that looks like a hump on their back, and have very long flippers. They breathe air with their lungs. They give birth to live young. Humpback whales have hair. They are a baleen whale and eat krill and plankton.

Class Model

HUMPBACK WHALE

Water is where they live

Hump is really a dorsal fin

Air is what they breathe

Long flippers

Eat krill and plankton

 ## Instructional Steps

Introduction

1. Explain to students that an acrostic fact poem is a poem that uses the letters in a word to write facts about that word. Each line begins with a letter from the word and the fact follows.

2. Model the acrostic poem with your name. For instance, Ms. Nye can be:

   Mighty good teacher

   Sweet as can be

   Nice to be around

   Youthful looking

   Energetic and likes to run

3. Have students write an acrostic poem with their name. Explain that the lines of the poem must describe them.

Teacher Modeling and Guided Practice

1. Tell students that together you will read a short text and write an acrostic fact poem about the topic.

2. Read the text aloud and identify the topic.

3. Write the topic name vertically on a chart or whiteboard.

4. Have students supply information about the topic for each line.

5. Read the resulting poem together.

Directions for Independent Application

1. Students refer to the assigned text and write the topic of the text vertically on their sheet of paper.

2. Students read the text and supply words or phrases for the acrostic poem on the topic word they selected.

 Taking Ownership

Explain to students that their acrostic fact poem is going to be displayed. Give students a large piece of light-colored or white paper. Using a ruler, students draw a "frame" in a color or design of their choice. Then students write their finalized acrostic fact poem in the frame. Allow students to add meaningful and purposeful pictures.

 Assessment

When assessing students' acrostic fact poems, ask yourself the following:

✔ Is the acrostic topic word spelled correctly?

✔ Is all the information correct?

✔ Did the student include enough information?

✔ Does the information correspond to the topic word?

 Differentiation

✦ To scaffold this task, give students a topic word to use for their acrostic. Have them write the letters to the topic word down the side of their paper in color using a crayon, colored pencil, or marker. Using the initial letters (the ones in color), students associate major words from their reading that begin with these letters. If needed and available, allow students to use the glossary from the informational text.

✦ To extend this task, have students use an Internet acrostic poem maker to create a poem on the computer.

 Variations

✦ Instead of writing the acrostic using the letters of a word, students use a sequence in the alphabet such as ABC or LMNOP for their topic-related words.

✦ Use a word that is associated with the main topic to write the acrostic fact poem. For example, suggest that students use *January* for facts about snow, *layers* for facts about the rainforest, or *trunk* for facts about an elephant.

Lesson 12

Description

 ## What Is It?

"Description" is a text structure that includes a topic and supporting details, and is widely used to present important information about a topic. Students list this important information in a description graphic organizer, which allows them to visualize how the information goes together. Because the topic is often stated in the first sentence of a text, the Description graphic organizer scaffolds students by having them place a main idea at the top of the organizer and list the details below. The description text structure often includes specific "signal words" that may indicate the text structure and cue that important information is about to be told. Common signal words for description include: *for example, characteristics, for instance, such as, like, including, to illustrate, most important, in addition, another, furthermore,* and *also.* Learning some of these signal words will aid students in recognizing the text structure.

 ## Why Use It?

Graphic organizers help students organize information as they read and write. Authors choose various text structures to convey informational text depending on their purpose and intention. The description text structure contains a main idea and supporting details. Identifying text structure aids the reader and increases comprehension because it shows how important ideas in the text are interrelated (Meyer & Ray, 2011). In addition, teaching students to understand text structure enables them to predict the pattern of the text. According to Ropič and Aberšek (2012), teaching students to recognize text structure allows them to predict what information the text will provide and which parts are more important.

 ## Text Selection

Select a text or section of text that is written in the description text structure, which begins with the main topic followed by details.

Instructional Steps

Introduction

1. Explain to students that the description text structure often begins with a topic sentence followed by supporting details. All the information in the passage supports and expands on the main topic.

2. Display an enlarged version of the Description graphic organizer. Explain to students that this graphic organizer will give them a visual picture of how the author organized his or her writing and that you will be filling one in together.

Teacher Modeling and Guided Practice

1. Read the passage together and decide what the main topic is. It may help to choose a text in which the main topic is written in bold. Write the main topic in its place on the graphic organizer.

Strategy *in Action*

Text

TORNADOES

A tornado is a very dangerous storm. Usually the United States has about 1,000 tornadoes a year. Tornadoes are made of air that rotates at a high speed and extends from the thunderstorm to the ground. They can travel as fast as 300 miles per hour and can do a lot of damage to property and people. Sometimes they destroy things within a mile-long path.

Class Model

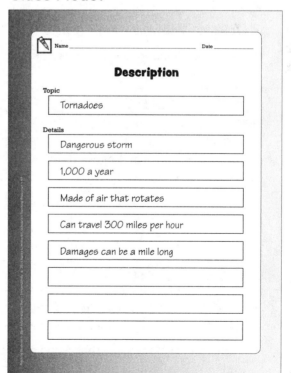

2. Reread the text and decide on the number of details that support the topic. Explain to students that they will fill in the boxes with the details. Some boxes may remain blank.

3. Have students give you supporting details as you fill in the detail boxes.

4. Once finished, check your original estimate of details to ensure you have included all of them. Have students check their detail list against the actual details in the text.

Directions for Independent Application

1. Group students in pairs to read and work together.

2. Distribute copies of the Description graphic organizer..

3. Students complete the graphic organizer with the next section of the text.

 ## Taking Ownership

Students choose the main idea and some details from their graphic organizer and summarize this section of reading. They also circle any signal words used in their writing. They can share their work in groups.

 ## Assessment

When assessing students' graphic organizers or summaries, ask yourself the following:

✔ Is all the information correct?

✔ Is the main idea of the topic clear?

✔ Did the student include enough details?

 ## Differentiation

✦ To scaffold this task, give students a highlighter or highlighter tape to identify the supporting details in the text. If necessary, decide together what should be written in the topic box.

✦ To extend this task, have students add to the Description graphic organizer by writing minor details under the main detail boxes.

 ## Variations

✦ Students draw a large umbrella near the top of their paper. On the umbrella they write the main topic. Under the umbrella students write the supporting details.

✦ Students create a graphic that represents the topic. For example, if the topic is bears, students could draw a bear and write a supporting detail on each paw.

Name _____ Date _____

Description

Topic

```
[                                                    ]
```

Details

```
[                                                    ]
```

```
[                                                    ]
```

```
[                                                    ]
```

```
[                                                    ]
```

```
[                                                    ]
```

```
[                                                    ]
```

```
[                                                    ]
```

```
[                                                    ]
```

Question-Answer

 ## What Is It?

While reading, students write questions and answers on a graphic organizer to help them understand the text structure and the information in the text. Often a question is in bold or used as a heading and can be easily identified. Finding the answer can be more complicated. Teach students how to select information to answer the question as directly as possible. In some texts, questions will be implicit and more difficult to identify. For these less visible questions, help students understand how the questions are hidden in the text and may not be written in typical form with a question mark. For example, the text may say, "The scientists were not sure how to produce synthetic gas" as opposed to "How do you produce synthetic gas?" Implicit questions can be similar to the statements in a problem-solution text structure.

 ## Why Use It?

It is well established that graphic organizers are a good tool for organizing information. The question-answer text structure can be complicated for some children to grasp. An answer may encompass numerous details. Writing notes in the graphic organizer helps students visualize and connect the questions and answers. According to Mills (2009), instruction in metacognitive strategies assists students in becoming effective learners. The author further states that metacognitive strategies, such as using knowledge of text structures, can be enhanced through training. Using a graphic organizer for question-answer texts can help students understand this text structure.

 ## Text Selection

Choose an informational text that is structured in a question-and-answer format. You may want to choose a text with a straightforward question, such as "What are endangered species?" The question-answer structured texts often have a series of questions followed by the answers.

Instructional Steps

Introduction

1. Show students a text in the question-and-answer format.

2. Explain that students are going to use a graphic organizer to take notes as they read.

3. Tell students that the first section of the graphic organizer will be the question.

Teacher Modeling and Guided Practice

1. Show students the text and point out the explicit question.

2. Display an enlarged version of the Question-Answer graphic organizer.

3. Explain to students that question, which in this case is the section title, goes on the top line.

Strategy *in Action*

Text

HOW DO SEEDS TRAVEL?

Seeds get from place to place in four different ways. Some seeds have wing-like shapes and can glide with the wind. Sometimes seeds get stuck on a boot or a sock and "hitchhike" to a different place. Some seeds can live in water and travel with the current of the water. Finally, sometimes animals eat seeds and, yep, you guessed it: The seeds come out fertilized, which helps them grow.

Class Model

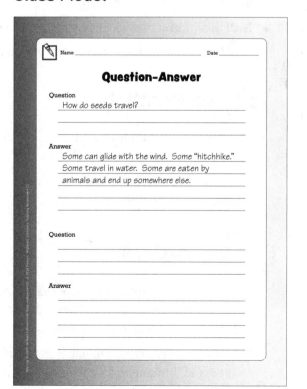

Name _____ Date _____

Question-Answer

Question
How do seeds travel?
_____
_____

Answer
Some can glide with the wind. Some "hitchhike."
Some travel in water. Some are eaten by
animals and end up somewhere else.
_____
_____

Question
_____
_____
_____

Answer
_____
_____
_____
_____

4. Read through the selection with students to find the answer. Write the answer in the appropriate section.

5. Go to the next question in the text, and continue as above.

Directions for Independent Application

1. Distribute copies of the Question-Answer graphic organizer.

2. As students begin to read the assigned text, have them show you the first question prior to writing it on the graphic organizer to be sure they understand the activity.

3. Students write down the questions and answers in the appropriate sections.

 ## Taking Ownership

Place students into collaborative groups. Using a game format, students take turns asking the questions they discovered within the text. The challenge is for the other students to identify and share the correct answers.

 ## Assessment

When assessing students' graphic organizers, ask yourself the following:

✔ Is the question stated correctly?

✔ Is all the information in the answer section correct and complete?

✔ Did the student include enough information in the answer?

 ## Differentiation

✦ To scaffold this task, check that students have written the correct question. Then have them use a highlighter or highlighter tape to show where the answer is located.

✦ To extend this task, have students write an additional question that could have been asked as the topic title.

 ## Variations

✦ Students cut out a question-mark shaped paper to put the question on and write the answer on an index card. They glue the question mark to the back of the index card and use it as a self-study note.

✦ Fold a sheet of construction paper in half and cut through the top layer to create flaps. Students write the question on the flap, then flip it open and write the answer inside.

Question-Answer

Question

_____

_____

_____

Answer

_____

_____

_____

_____

_____

Question

_____

_____

_____

Answer

_____

_____

_____

_____

MEETING THE
COMMON
CORE

RI.3.5   RI.4.5   RI.5.5

Sequential Order

 ## What Is It?

As students read, they fill out a graphic organizer to show the sequence of events. As they pay attention to how and why events occur in a particular order, their comprehension will increase. In addition, students look for specific signal words that are used in sequentially written text, such as *first, second, third, later, next, before, then, finally, after, when, since, now, previously, initially,* and *not long after.*

 ## Why Use It?

By following a sequence of events in a text, a reader can see how the information is connected. According to Meyer and Ray (2011), focusing on text structure helps readers organize concepts of implied and explicit relationships within a text, which aids students' comprehension. In chronological or sequential order, each step is dependent on the next. Using a graphic organizer to help teach the sequential text structure gives students a visual of the connections, making it easier for students to build memory representations and recall information. When reading about an event that took place over a span of months or years, students are better able to grasp the timing and order of the event if they write down the information in a list.

 ## Text Selection

The text used for this activity must be written in either sequential or chronological order. To introduce this activity, choose a text written chronologically. Once students understand the activity, you can use a more complex text, in which an author might write about something happening on September 18th and then discuss a previous event that happened in June. Do not use a text that simply enumerates events.

Instructional Steps

Introduction

1. Tell students that the order of events is very important in some texts and explain why. For instance, if the text discusses the life stages of an animal, we would want to know them in the correct order so that we can fully understand the development process.

2. Ask students to share their routines of getting ready for school. Some eat breakfast first, then get dressed; others may do things in a different order. Listen to the students' words and highlight some of the signal words they say, such as *first, then,* or *next.*

3. Discuss the signal words that we use to show the sequence of events.

Strategy *in Action*

Text

THE WATER CYCLE

Precipitation is water in the form of snow, rain, sleet, or even hail. First, the precipitation falls from the clouds to the ground. Then, the water runs into streams, rivers, lakes, and oceans. Next, the water begins to evaporate back to the sky. Finally, when the water vapor collects in the sky, it forms clouds. This is called condensation. Then the cycle begins again.

Class Model

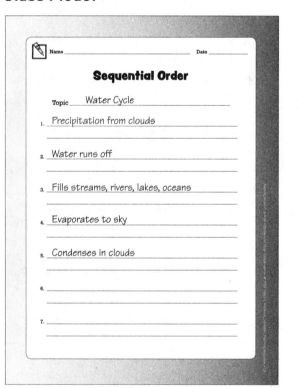

Teacher Modeling and Guided Practice

1. Project the text on a screen or hand each student a copy.

2. Point out the sequential order of the text, whether that sequence stems from time or events.

3. Before you read the text say, "Everyone should be listening and looking for signal words that tell you when something is being done." Tell students to look for the following signal words: *first, second, third, later, next, before, then, finally, after, when, since, now, previously, initially,* and *not long after.* In addition, tell students that dates can also signal an order.

4. Read the text together and underline all the signal words. If underlining is not possible, students will need to write the list of words or use highlighter tape.

5. Using the clues from the signal words, fill in the Sequential Order graphic organizer.

6. Discuss the order of events and ask students how one event might have led to or impacted the next.

Directions for Independent Application

1. Distribute copies of the Sequential Order graphic organizer.

2. Students read the selection with a partner and fill in the Sequential Order graphic organizer.

3. Explain that if there are just a few steps, it may not be necessary to fill in every section on the organizer. Also, if there are more steps than space allows on the graphic organizer, students should add more steps to the back of the page.

 Taking Ownership

Place students in pairs to compare the order of events written on their graphic organizers. If there are any discrepancies between their graphic organizers, students should use the "look back" strategy and refer to the text to decide the correct sequence. Have students discuss how the events impacted each other.

Assessment

When assessing students' graphic organizers, ask yourself the following:

✔ Is the order of events correct?

✔ Is the information complete and correct?

✔ Are there an appropriate number of steps?

Differentiation

✦ To scaffold this task, highlight or underline the signal words with students. Then have them complete the graphic organizer.

✦ To extend this task, have students write between the events on the graphic organizer how each event impacted the following event.

Variations

✦ Have students fold over the top of a piece of paper to create a small section for the title. Create additional sections so that there is one for each event. For instance, if there are three main events, the students should fold the rest of the paper twice more to make a total of four sections. Students can write the topic, then one event in each section of the paper.

✦ Students use strips of paper. They write the topic on one strip and the events on the others then put them in order. Working with a collaborative group, students glue the strips to a sheet of paper once the group has agreed the events are in order.

Name _____ Date _____

Sequential Order

Topic _____

1. _____

_____

2. _____

_____

3. _____

_____

4. _____

_____

5. _____

_____

6. _____

_____

7. _____

_____

RI.3.5   RI.4.5   RI.5.5

Compare and Contrast

What Is It?

Compare and contrast text structure is used when authors want to show differences and similarities between two or more things, such as objects, people, places, events, and ideas. Using a Venn diagram, students organize facts to compare and contrast two subjects in the text. Students also look for specific signal words that are used when comparing and contrasting, such as *however, nevertheless, on the other hand, but, similarly, just like, just as, likewise, in comparison, whereas, yet, although, also, in contrast, different, alike, same as, as opposed to,* and *unless.*

Why Use It?

Authors of informational texts use the compare and contrast text structure to discuss information about two or more items when a comparison is important to the information being portrayed. Teaching text structure increases comprehension as readers learn to use cues inherent in well-structured text (Williams, et al., 2009). Studies have shown that students who receive instruction in the compare and contrast text structure show greater understanding of what they read than those who do not (Williams et al., 2005). A Venn diagram provides readers with a visual that organizes the information into categories: *alike* and *different.* The visual makes it easier for students to glean the main ideas from the text.

Text Selection

Choose a text with a compare and contrast text structure. A short selection from a longer text will work well. Use a text selection that incorporates signal words.

⟳ Instructional Steps

Introduction

1. Hold up a pen and pencil and ask students how the writing utensils are alike and how they are different. Sample answers: They both write, but the pencil mark can be erased; marks from both can smudge, but the ink isn't erasable.

2. Explain that when we talk about how things are alike and different we are comparing and contrasting.

3. Explain to students that signal words can give us a clue that things are being compared. Give the students a list of common signal words for compare and contrast: *however, nevertheless, on the other hand, but, similarly, just like, just as, likewise, in comparison, whereas, yet, although, also, in contrast, different, alike, same as, as opposed to,* and *unless.*

Teacher Modeling and Guided Practice

1. Tell students they will be reading a text that compares and contrasts items.

2. To begin, display this paragraph on the board:

   > Tom and Paul were not only brothers, but best friends. Unlike Tom, Paul was short. Tom had light blue eyes just like his brother's. Tom's hair was blond, whereas Paul's was brown.

3. Read the sentences and ask students to describe Paul. Then ask students to describe Tom.

4. When students describe Tom as tall, say, "How did you know Tom is tall?" Discuss how the word *unlike* signals a difference. Underline the word *unlike.*

5. Ask students to look for other signal words in the paragraph (*unlike, just like,* and *whereas*). As signal words are identified underline them. Discuss how these words signal that something is the same or different. Ask students which words signaled that something was the same (*just like*).

6. Using the information from the paragraph, fill out a Venn diagram while explaining the process to students.

7. Pass out or display the list of possible signal words.

8. Display the sample text. As you read it with students, ask them to raise their hand when you come to a signal word. Underline the word and ask if the word implies that something is alike or different.

Strategy *in Action*

Text

Largest and Smallest States

Alaska is the largest state in the United States of America. The capital of Alaska is Juneau, but the largest city is Anchorage. Alaska gets snow and has a long winter season. Alaska borders the ocean. The population of Alaska is about 630,000 people. Alaska's nickname is "The Last Frontier."

On the other hand, Rhode Island is the smallest state in the union. The capital is Providence and that is the largest city in Rhode Island. Rhode Island gets snow, but unlike in Alaska, winter is not long. Rhode Island borders the ocean. The population of Rhode Island is over one million people. The state's nickname is "The Ocean State" although some people call it "Little Rhody."

Class Model

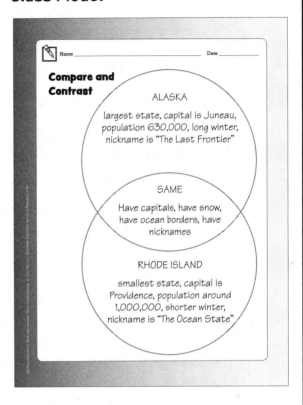

9. Have students help you fill out a Venn diagram using evidence from the text. Once again, discuss the process.

Directions for Independent Application

1. Distribute copies of the Compare and Contrast graphic organizer.

2. In pairs, students read and fill out the Venn diagram on the assigned text.

3. Remind students to look for signal words.

Taking Ownership

Create collaborative groups of four and ask students to discuss the similarities and differences of a text. For this discussion, students identify the most important difference and explain why they think this difference is important.

Assessment

When assessing students' graphic organizers, ask yourself the following:

✔ Is all the information correct?

✔ Has the student written all the important information?

✔ Is the information in the proper place in the Venn diagram?

Differentiation

◆ To scaffold this task, have students use a T-Chart instead of the Venn diagram. Tell students to label one column of the T-Chart *alike* and the other column *different*. Have students fill in the columns with information from the text.

◆ To extend this task, have students revisit the Venn diagram to identify and write the categories used for comparing and contrasting. For instance, if two U.S. presidents are being compared, the Venn diagram might have the towns where they grew up, the colleges where they studied, whether they were in Congress, and a number of other attributes. Students would look at the information in the Venn diagram and label the categories being compared.

Variations

◆ Students read a text that compares three different items. Then they use a tri-circle graphic organizer to compare and contrast the items.

◆ Students cut out three same-size circles and punch a hole at the top of all three. Students label two of the circles with the two different items that are being compared and the word *different*. They write the word *same* on the third circle. The circles become the three pieces of the Venn diagram. Students fill in the circles and use a brad to put them together. They can swing the circles open to see how the items are different and alike.

Name _____ Date _____

Compare and Contrast

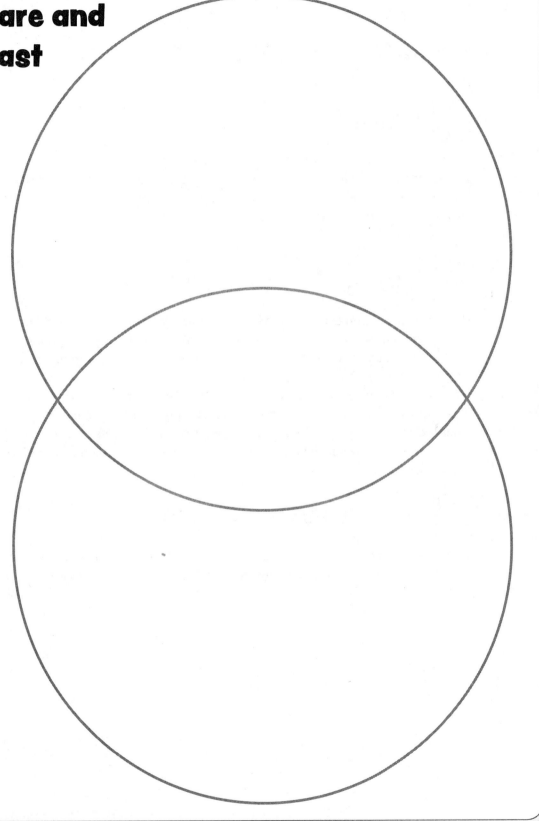

Problem-Solution

 ## What Is It?

As students read, they identify and write down main problems and solutions on a graphic organizer, which contains room for more than one solution. In addition, students look for specific signal words used in problem-solution text structure, such as *the problem is, if/then, because, so that, the dilemma is, question/answer, solved, solution,* or *the answer is.*

 ## Why Use It?

The problem-solution text structure is used in both narrative and informational text, albeit for different purposes. Studies have found that because the problem-solution text structure is a more organized text structure than description, it allows readers to have better recall. In addition, text signaling devices (signal words) aid in recall of information (Ray and Meyer, 2011). As students learn to analyze text structure, they begin to show a greater understanding of the concepts within the text. When working with the problem-solution text structure, students focus on two pieces of information (the problem and solution) and are able to make connections between that information.

 ## Text Selection

Select a text or section of text with the problem-solution text structure. To introduce this activity, you might choose to use a text that explicitly states, "The problem was . . ."

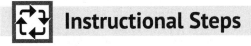 **Instructional Steps**

Introduction

1. Say to students, "I have a problem. I have a sock with a hole in it, what can I do?"

2. Have students generate solutions: sew the sock, use fabric glue to mend the sock, match it with another sock, wear socks that don't match, wear the sock with the hole, or throw the sock away.

3. Discuss how problems can often have one or more solutions, in life and in books.

4. Explain that students are going to be looking for problems and solutions in the text they are reading.

5. Tell students some signal words that suggest problem-solution text structure: *the problem is, if/then, because, so that, the dilemma is, question/answer, solved, solution,* or *the answer is.*

Teacher Modeling and Guided Practice

1. Say to students, "Sometimes authors use a problem-solution text structure to write because they want readers to know that a problem existed and the solution was found for that problem. We are going to read together to see if we can identify the problem and solution."

2. Display an enlarged version the Problem-Solution graphic organizer.

3. Before reading, remind students of the possible signal words that may be found in a text with the problem-solution text structure.

4. Read through the text with students and identify the problem together, then write the problem on the organizer. When writing the problem, explain to students that you should include who or what has the problem.

5. Continue reading the text to find the solution, once again pointing out signal words. Write the solution in the designated spot on the graphic organizer.

6. Hold a discussion with the class and, if possible, generate alternative solutions to the problem.

Directions for Independent Application

1. Distribute copies of the Problem-Solution graphic organizer.

2. As students read the assigned text, they fill in the graphic organizer.

3. Remind students to pay attention to signal words.

Strategy *in Action*

Text

Many years ago, during World War II, brown tree snakes were accidently brought to the island of Guam. This caused a very serious problem in Guam's ecosystem. Since their arrival, the brown tree snakes have eaten many of the native forest birds, especially the beloved koko birds. There are so many brown tree snakes in one highly populated section of the jungle, there are said to be 20 snakes per acre.

Scientists have found that acetaminophen, a pain reliever that is in some headache medicines, is deadly to brown tree snakes. To solve the problem, in 2010 scientists started introducing mice that have been injected with acetaminophen into the highly populated area in the jungle. Since snakes eat mice, this may be part of a solution to the problem.

Class Model

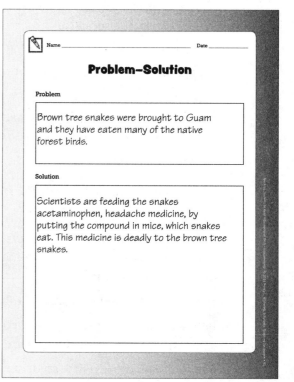

Name _____ Date _____

Problem–Solution

Problem

Brown tree snakes were brought to Guam and they have eaten many of the native forest birds.

Solution

Scientists are feeding the snakes acetaminophen, headache medicine, by putting the compound in mice, which snakes eat. This medicine is deadly to the brown tree snakes.

Taking Ownership

After completing their graphic organizer, students check to see if the problem could have, or should have, been solved differently. They write down their reasoning and also circle any signal words they have used.

 ## Assessment

When assessing students' graphic organizers, ask yourself the following:

✔ Is all the information correct?

✔ Are the problem and solution(s) clear?

✔ Are both the problem and the solution(s) complete?

 ## Differentiation

✦ To scaffold this task, discuss the problem with students. Have students read and identify the solution on their own.

✦ To extend this task, have students write the problem, solution, who or what impacted the problem, and whether anything could have been done to avoid the problem.

 ## Variations

✦ Assign partners. One of the students writes a letter about the problem in the text. The other student answers the letter by giving the solution from the text to solve the problem.

✦ Students create questions in a game-like format under two categories: *problem* or *solution*. Each student reads a question and other students identify if the question is part of the problem or the solution.

Name _____ Date _____

Problem–Solution

Problem

```
┌─────────────────────────────────────────┐
│                                         │
│                                         │
│                                         │
│                                         │
│                                         │
└─────────────────────────────────────────┘
```

Solution

```
┌─────────────────────────────────────────┐
│                                         │
│                                         │
│                                         │
│                                         │
│                                         │
│                                         │
│                                         │
│                                         │
│                                         │
└─────────────────────────────────────────┘
```

Lesson 17

Cause and Effect

 ## What Is It?

Students identify causes and effects as they read and fill in a graphic organizer that shows the trail from cause to effect. Cause and effect, in its simplest form, is a relationship between an outcome (effect) and the conditions (cause) that caused the outcome. Make students aware that in a cause-and-effect relationship there is usually a trail, as one effect can then create another condition or cause. In addition, students should look for specific signal words that allow them to identify the cause-and-effect text structure, such as *because, since, if/then, as a result, this led to, so, for this reason, thus, nevertheless, due to, therefore, may be due to, reasons why, hence, consequently,* and *so that.*

 ## Why Use It?

Although it is an organized text structure that follows a sequence, cause-and-effect text structure can be very difficult to recognize. There may actually be multiple causes and effects in a sequence. To further complicate matters, effects can become causes creating a trail within the text, which makes it difficult for a reader to comprehend. Studies have shown that teaching text structure and using graphic organizers to support that teaching is beneficial (Read, Reutzel, and Fawson, 2008). In addition, teaching cause-and-effect text structure helps students identify the main idea and supporting details. Marinak (2008) states that in the cause-and-effect text structure, supporting details are often the causes of the major idea (effect).

 ## Text Selection

Texts selected for this activity must have the cause-and-effect text structure. This structure is sometimes hard to recognize and is usually embedded in a description text structure.

Introduction

1. Show students a picture of a T-shirt with two smeared paint stains. Explain that when you were painting, a spot of paint got on your clothing when you hit it with the wet paintbrush. You tried to rub off the paint with your fingers, but the stain got bigger and you ended up with paint on your fingers, too. When you went to wash your fingers, you hit your shirt with your fingers and ended up with a second paint stain.

2. Ask students what caused the first paint stain (the brush) and what effect that had on what you did (tried to rub off the stain with your fingers).

3. Ask what you had to do to get the paint off your fingers (went to wash) and what that caused (a second paint stain).

Strategy *in Action*

Text

The temperature and moisture from warm ocean waters and a colder air system mix to create the swirling motion that we call a hurricane. When a hurricane reaches land, not only does it bring winds of 120 miles or more, but it also causes a storm surge of water to come on land.

The wind and water from the hurricane cause a lot of damage to businesses and homes. People must move elsewhere until homes are rebuilt, and businesses sometimes have to close. Volunteers and workers travel to the hurricane site to aid in the rebuilding. Sometimes the recovery from a hurricane takes many years.

Class Model

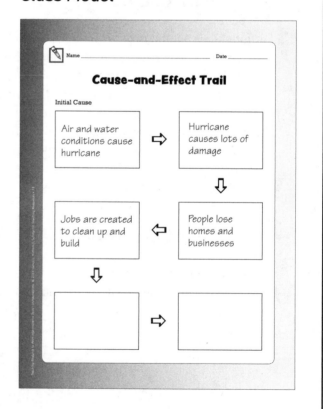

4. Tell students that this is called cause and effect and that cause-and-effect events are commonly found in texts.

5. Discuss the concept of a cause-and-effect relationship, explaining that we can tell causes and effects through details in the text.

6. Tell students that there are signal words within a text that hint at the cause-and-effect relationship, such as *since, because, consequently, but/then, therefore,* and *as a result of.*

Teacher Modeling and Guided Practice

1. Display the following scenario on the board:

> Let's pretend we woke up in the morning and there were two feet of fresh snow on the ground. Since this makes traveling to school dangerous, school was cancelled. On this particular "snow day," there was supposed to be a program on reptiles. Consequently, that had to be rescheduled for the next week. Unfortunately, the program had to be scheduled during our music time, therefore we had to miss music class.

2. Read the text to students and underline the signal words (*since, consequently, therefore*).

3. Display an enlarged version of the Cause-and-Effect Trail graphic organizer. Show students the trail of cause and effect, as follows:

> Two feet of snow ▶ school was cancelled ▶ program was rescheduled ▶ music class was missed

4. Mention to students that not all the boxes were filled in because that was the end of the effects in the text. (There could potentially be more, such as the music teacher putting up a new bulletin board because she did not teach the class.)

Directions for Independent Application

1. Distribute copies of the Cause-and-Effect Trail graphic organizer.

2. Group students in reading pairs and assign the cause-and-effect text.

3. Begin reading with students and help them identify the first cause.

4. Partners read and continue to fill out the graphic organizer.

Taking Ownership

Place reading partner teams together with another set of reading partners, so the group has four. Have the teams confer that the causes and effects are correct.

 Assessment

When assessing students' graphic organizers, ask yourself the following:

✔ Is all the information correct?

✔ Is the cause-and-effect trail in sequential order?

✔ Are all the pieces of the cause-and-effect trail in place?

 Differentiation

✦ To scaffold this task, give students a cause-and-effect trail with the cause "blocks" filled in. Tell them to focus on the effects of the causes as they read and complete the blocks.

✦ To extend this task, have students go beyond the text. Using what has happened in the text, have students write a possible next effect. For instance, if a flood caused home destruction and a dam was built to stop this ask, "What effect could the dam have—to wildlife, fish, or people?"

 Variations

✦ Students use visuals to create a cause-and-effect map that shows the relationship between the two.

✦ Students create a cause-and-effect web to show that one cause may result in multiple cause-and-effect trails.

Name _____ Date _____

Cause-and-Effect Trail

Initial Cause

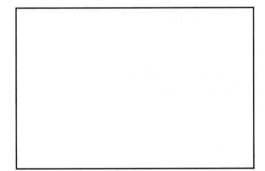 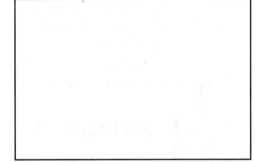

MEETING THE
COMMON
CORE

RI.3.4   RI.4.4   RI.5.4

Shape Poetry

 What Is It?

In this activity, students write down or underline domain-specific vocabulary and main ideas from the text. They think about pictures or objects that represent the ideas in the text, then write the words and phrases they selected in the shape of one of those objects. For example, facts about the three branches of government could be written in the shape of a courthouse or the shape of the American flag.

 Why Use It?

Selecting domain-specific words and identifying main ideas are the focus of this activity. Being able to decide on an image or picture that represents the reading selection helps students think deeply about content and vocabulary. According to Leopold & Leutner (2012), when students connect the information in the text with a visual representation, they gain a greater understanding of the material. Shape poetry, also known as concrete poetry, is one way to visually represent the material. Using poetry to summarize content-area material gives students an opportunity to create meaning and improve their understanding of the concepts within the material (Szabo, 2008).

 Text Selection

The text for this activity should include abundant vocabulary that supports the main idea. The content should also bring to mind concrete pictures. The object of this exercise is for students to retain information, not struggle with abstract representations.

Instructional Steps

Introduction

1. Explain to students what shape poetry is and how it represents the main ideas in the text. For instance, they could write a poem to a loved one by writing nice things about them in a heart shape.

2. Show students a picture of a shape poem. (An online image search for "shape poem" or "concrete poem" brings up a variety of examples.)

3. Explain to students that shape poems use words that are associated with the picture.

4. Tell students they will be writing a shape poem on a topic they are studying.

Teacher Modeling and Guided Practice

1. Select a short content-area text that can be easily represented by at least three images. For instance, the solar system could be represented by a sphere, a star, or a rocket ship.

2. Project the reading material and say to students, "As we read this together, we want to underline important vocabulary and important phrases that give big ideas about the topic."

3. Read the text with students and ask for their input for underlining.

4. Ask students what shape might represent the topic of the passage. Write down their ideas on a chart and then decide as a class which shape to use.

5. Lightly outline the selected shape on the board or chart paper and model filling in the shape with the underlined words and phrases in the text.

6. Explain to students that they will be doing this with their assigned reading. If underlining is not possible, students will need to write the list of words and phrases to be used or use highlighter tape.

Directions for Independent Application

1. Assign students text to be read and discuss possible shapes for the topic.

2. Students underline, highlight, or make a list of the domain-specific words as they read.

3. When students have finished reading, they make a shape poem with the selected words.

Text

LIGHTNING

Lightning is made of electricity. Lightning happens during a thunderstorm and can be very dangerous. In the clouds way up in the sky tiny pieces of ice bump into each other, and this creates an electrical charge. These charges become positive and negative at each end, kind of like in a magnet. The negative charge faces the earth and causes a positive charge to build up on the earth on something that is above the ground, like a tree or people. The two charges attract each other. When they connect, lightning is made.

Class Model

Lightning! Thunderstorm! Tiny pieces of ice bump. Create an electrical charge. Negative charge faces the earth, positive charge builds up on the earth— Lightning is made!

 ## Taking Ownership

Place students in collaborative groups. Students read their shape poem to their group and explain how their shape is representative of the text.

 ## Assessment

When assessing students' shape poems, ask yourself the following:

✔ Does the shape represent the topic?

✔ Is all the information correct?

✔ Are domain-specific words and main concepts included?

Differentiation

+ To scaffold this task, either discuss representative shapes with students or hand out copies of a lightly drawn representative shape they can write the words on.

+ To extend this task, have students draw at least three shapes. Each shape must contain a different concept from within the text. In essence, this shape poetry would be concept mapping.

Variations

+ Students lightly draw a shape on a piece of paper. The shape should be about three-fourths the size of the paper. Students write words and phrases randomly over the page, so the lightly drawn shape becomes interesting background.

+ Students use colored pencils or thin markers to write the words and phrases on the shape. They put a complete phrase in one color. To increase the artistic effect, encourage students to use colors that may represent the concept, such as red and blue for the United States, or red and black for a volcano.

Four-Square Summary

 ## What Is It?

Students use the Four-Square Summary graphic organizer to organize main points and domain-specific vocabulary. As they read, students write the following in the first three boxes: (1) main ideas, (2) details, and (3) domain-specific words with contextual definitions. After reading, students use the notes from the first three squares to write a short summary in the remaining square. In the Four-Square Summary, domain-specific words should actually appear in multiple squares as students use the words in different ways.

 ## Why Use It?

In this activity, students identify main ideas, match the main ideas with supporting details, and select domain-specific words. When thinking about an overall concept, domain-specific words cannot completely be separated from the main ideas. According to Baumann and Graves (2010), it is crucial for learners to acquire domain-specific vocabulary knowledge in order to understand the knowledge from that domain. According to Bintz (2011), students must be offered strategies that focus not only on word recognition, but also on using the word in meaningful contexts to have the most effect on vocabulary growth.

 ## Text Selection

The text for this activity should contain important domain-specific words. A text in which the domain-specific words are in bold will make identifying key vocabulary easier for students.

Instructional Steps

Introduction

1. Tell students they will be using a Four-Square Summary graphic organizer to write down notes as they read.

2. Discuss the squares: Main Ideas, Supporting Details, Vocabulary Words, and Summary.

Strategy *in Action*

Text

THE GREAT DEPRESSION

The Great Depression happened in the 1930s. It was hard economic times. Money was scarce and there were very few jobs. People in the United States and throughout the world could not afford to buy things that they needed, even food.

The Depression started when the stock market crashed on Black Tuesday, October 29, 1929. Business stocks became worth very little or nothing and thousands of people lost their money. The stock market crash caused people to lose their jobs. When people lost their jobs, they could not afford to pay their rent or house mortgage and whole families became homeless.

Class Model

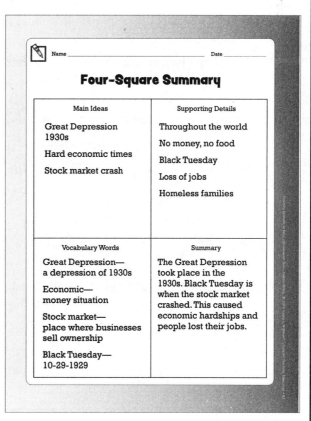

Teacher Modeling and Guided Practice

1. Select a short content-area text.

2. Discuss main ideas, supporting details, and content-area vocabulary.

3. Display an enlarged version of the Four-Square Summary graphic organizer and project the text.

4. Say to students, "As we read, we are going to be thinking about what to write in three of the squares. In the top left square we will write main ideas. In the top right square we will write the supporting details for the main ideas. In the bottom left square we will write the content vocabulary words and define them. After reading, we will write a short summary in the last square."

5. As you read, identify main ideas, supporting details, and content vocabulary, and write them in the assigned squares.

6. When writing the supporting details, align the details with the corresponding main idea. Explain to students that this is being done to help keep the ideas clear and connected.

7. When writing the content words and definitions, work with the class to construct a definition from the context.

8. When notes are completed, tell students that the notes will be used to write the summary in the last square. As a class, write a short summary of the content.

Directions for Independent Application

1. Distribute copies of the Four-Square Summary graphic organizer.

2. Students use the graphic organizer with their assigned reading.

3. Remind students to align supporting details with the corresponding main idea.

 ## Taking Ownership

Students finish the activity by writing a two- or three-sentence summary using the information from the other three boxes. The summary is written in the fourth box.

Assessment

When assessing students' Four-Square Summaries, ask yourself the following:

✔ Is all the information correct?

✔ Are domain-specific words and correct definitions included?

✔ Are the main ideas separated from the details correctly?

Differentiation

✦ To scaffold this task, have students begin with two "squares". Have them fold a piece of paper in half. In one section, students write the main ideas, in the other the domain-specific vocabulary. Students then summarize orally in teams.

✦ To extend this task, have students use the back of the four-square paper to do the following: In the top left square draw a picture or diagram representing the topic; in the top right square write what they felt was most interesting about the topic; in the bottom left square write questions they still have about the topic; in the bottom right square list topics that are related in some way, such as federal government to state government.

Variations

✦ Create a four-flap lift "book" out of construction paper, using the four flaps as you would the four squares of the graphic organizer.

✦ Students narrow the focus of their four squares to domain-specific vocabulary. Students choose four vocabulary words as they read and put one in each box with a definition.

Name _____ Date _____

Four-Square Summary

Main Ideas	Supporting Details

Vocabulary Words	Summary

Lesson 20

Word Splash

 ## What Is It?

Students use a word splash program, such as Wordle, to make a word splash with domain-specific words they choose. As students read, they write down five to eight important or interesting words from the text, what they think the words mean, and in what context the words might be used. It is important to note that if students include content-area phrases, the program will separate these into individual words for the word splash. (The computer must have Java to work with Wordle.)

 ## Why Use It?

Word splashes are mostly a motivational activity, although the act of typing the correct spelling reinforces word recognition. In addition, word association helps students to remember information. Of academic importance is the selection of domain-specific words and applying context clues to figure out word meaning. It is well documented that students learn most words through wide reading. In addition, word knowledge grows over time and is not an "all or nothing phenomenon" (Stahl and Bravo, 2010, p 567). Beck, McKeown, and Kucan (2002) explain that students gain increased knowledge of a word as they obtain more exposure to the word. Using context to gain word meaning aids students in both understanding the word more thoroughly as they encounter it, and placing the word into their expressive vocabulary.

 ## Text Selection

This activity works with any informational text, but a text with rich vocabulary will be most effective. The vocabulary should stand alone and describe the topic through verbs and details.

Instructional Steps

Introduction

1. Prior to the lesson, make a word splash with words describing you.

2. Share your word splash and tell students that the topic is you, and all the words in the word splash describe you in some way.

3. Tell students they are going to make a word splash describing the topic of their reading.

Teacher Modeling and Guided Practice

1. Use a short content-area text to show students how to select words they don't know or that are domain-specific words about the topic.

2. Display the text and, as you read, do a think aloud. For instance, if your topic is the heart, you might select words like *veins, blood, blue, transport, ventricles, aorta,* and *muscle.*

Strategy *in Action*

Text

IGNEOUS ROCKS

One type of rock is an igneous rock. There are many kinds of igneous rocks. Igneous rocks can be made from volcanoes. Volcanoes spurt out magma. Magma is molten or melted rock that exists below the earth's surface. As the magma cools it becomes crystallized. This means that the elements in the magma bond together. Two kinds of igneous rocks that are formed from magma are lava, a grayish rock that often has hole-like features, and granite, a rock that is very hard and contains light and dark colors.

Class Model

IGNEOUS ROCKS

igneous—rock from magma

magma—molten or melted rock that exists below the earth's surface

crystallize—make into a rock

bond—stick together

lava—gray rock with holes

granite—hard rock with light and dark colors

3. In this think aloud, you could say, "I have heard the word *vein* before because when the nurse checks my blood, she takes a sample from my vein. So I know it has something to do with blood. I see in the diagram that the veins are blue. Oh, it says in the text that a vein transports blood to the heart. I am going to underline the word *vein* as that is important and the word *transport*. Since the vein transports blood to the heart, I think transport means that it carries blood through the vein to the heart."

4. Label chart paper with the word *heart,* then write the word *vein* and a proposed definition. Do the same with *transport*. Continue with this method until the article is complete.

5. Your finished chart should contain all necessary vocabulary from the text and the definitions, as either defined in the text or gleaned by context clues.

6. Go to a word splash program on the Internet, such as Wordle at www.wordle.net/ to see some samples of Wordles created by others. Click on the Create tab.

7. Type in the words that you and the class selected to create a word splash.

Directions for Independent Application

1. As students read the assigned text they select their own content words or words that they need to define.

2. Students write down the words and a proposed meaning.

3. Students create a word splash.

4. They may save and print their word splashes to share.

 Taking Ownership

Students share their word splash and definition list with a small group. If students are lacking words, they may decide to add words to their paper. Students discuss their words' definitions. If they do not agree on a definition, they circle the word and discuss it as a class.

 Assessment

When assessing students' word splash and written list, ask yourself the following:

✔ Are the word choices appropriate for the content?

✔ Are the definitions correct and based on context?

✔ Are the important domain-specific words included?

Differentiation

✦ To scaffold this task, work with students in a small group to identify important domain-specific words. In the group, discuss possible meanings. Have students write the meanings independently.

✦ To extend this task, allow students time with a computer word splash program to create the word splash in different formats.

Variations

✦ Students write down complete phrases from the text. When the word splash is created the words will be separated. Students circle words that belong together with the same color. For instance, the phrase "veins carry blood" might be circled in blue.

✦ Students make the word splash by hand, using paper and markers or crayons.

MEETING THE **COMMON CORE**

RI.3.5 RI.4.5 RI.5.5

Grasping the Graphics

 ## What Is It?

In this activity, students focus their attention on the graphics in the informational text. Prior to reading the selection, students write down a description of each graphic in the text on the left side of a T-chart, making sure to include important domain-specific words. After reading the selection, students use the right side of the T-chart to write their opinion about the usefulness of the graphic and how the graphic helped them understand the information in the text.

 ## Why Use It?

Text features that are to the point and clearly related to the content can be extremely helpful to comprehension. In recent years, visual information, including images, diagrams, and maps in informational textbooks and trade books has increased (Coleman, Bradley, and Donovan, 2012). Previewing the material with a text-feature walk helps students reduce content into manageable chunks (Kelley and Clausen-Grace, 2010).

 ## Text Selection

Take care to select a text with effective graphics. The information in the graphics must align with or complement the information in the text. Use a short content-area text that includes visual images, such as maps, graphs, and photographs or illustrations with captions.

 ## Instructional Steps

Introduction

1. Say to students, "Pictures and other graphics in texts often help us understand what the text is telling us. We need to use them to help us understand."

2. Explain that the class will be working on getting information from graphics, including pictures and captions, in the text.

3. Explain that a caption is the writing underneath a picture.

Teacher Modeling and Guided Practice

1. Tell students they are going to do a "text-feature walk" to look at all the visual images the author has placed in the reading selection.

2. Project the text and do a think-aloud as you read. Look at each graphic and discuss its content.

3. Draw a large T-chart on the board; label the left side "Graphics" and the right side "Helpfulness."

4. On the left side, write a short note explaining each graphic as you talk about it. For instance, viewing the Food Guide Pyramid (visual graphic to recommended daily food choices), you might say, "It shows six food groups: bread, vegetable, fruit, milk, meat, and oils. It also says how much of each we should eat."

5. Continue with this process until you have previewed all graphics in the selection, then read the text.

6. Look back at your notes on the T-chart. Discuss whether each graphic helped you understand the reading. On the right side, write *yes* or *no* and explain.

Strategy *in Action*

Text

THE EARTH'S LAYERS

Our planet is made of many layers. The outer layer of the earth is called the crust. Underneath the crust, the next layer is called the mantle, which is made up of solid rock-like material. After that, comes the outer core, which is made of molten lava. Finally, in the middle of the earth is the inner core. The inner core is thought to be a big solid ball in the middle of the earth made of iron or another strong metal.

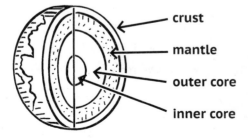

crust
mantle
outer core
inner core

Class Model

Graphics	Helpfulness
Layers of Earth • Crust • Mantle • Outer core • Inner core	Yes, picture helps because I can see where each layer is in the Earth.

Directions for Independent Application

1. Students fold a piece of lined paper in half to create their T-chart.
2. Students follow the T-chart format with their own reading.
3. Together, write the information needed for the first graphic.
4. Students continue looking through the graphics in the book, then read the selection and decide whether each graphic was helpful or not.

 Taking Ownership

Students work with a partner to ascertain that they have included every graphic and its important information.

 Assessment

When assessing students' T-charts, ask yourself the following:

✔ Are all the graphics included?

✔ Is all the information correct?

✔ Are domain-specific words included?

 Differentiation

✦ To scaffold this task, give students a T-chart with the graphics identified and labeled on the left side. Students add additional information from the graphics, and continue on with the reading.

✦ To extend this task, have students complete the assignment, then choose one of the graphics in the text and represent its information differently. For example, for the food pyramid, a student may decide to use a circle graph representation.

 Variations

✦ Students write a summary of the text then create a graphic that clarifies the information in the summary.

✦ Students create a concept web that connects textual information to the information from the graphic or picture.

Meeting the COMMON CORE

RI.3.5   RI.4.5   RI.5.5

Concept Mapping

What Is It?

Using the Description graphic organizer from Lesson 12, students write down key ideas and details from the text as they are reading. When finished, they use the information to create a concept map, or web. There are many free webbing tools online where students can type information into shapes that can be added, deleted, and moved easily. The shapes can be connected with arrows to create multiple connections. When completed, the concept web can be printed.

Why Use It?

Concept mapping is similar to the way we think. The visual representation of relationships among ideas on concept map is a lot like what goes on when we make connections in our mind. Concept mapping offers a visual strategy for enriching the understanding of a concept (Toolbox, *Reading Teacher*, 2011). They help students who might otherwise be too overwhelmed to organize information. According to Boulware and Crow (2008) the concept-mapping strategy is beneficial to students because it allows students to construct meaning through association and increases their comprehension from a multiple perspective.

Text Selection

Most general informational text can be used for this activity. Texts with bold headings will aid students in identifying main ideas by which to cluster their concept map.

Instructional Steps

Introduction

1. Explain to students that a concept map is a group of word webs that are connected in some way and that each cluster in a concept map is like a mini-word web.

2. To explain this process further, create a concept map using games as an example. Write *games* at the center of the map, then work with students to create a cluster, such as *video, outdoor, board,* and *team.* From there let the students brainstorm what might connect to each cluster.

Teacher Modeling and Guided Practice

1. Using the sample text provided, display an Internet-based program so students can build the concept map with you. The ReadWriteThink Webbing Tool, which is found at ReadWriteThink.org, allows students to create circles and type in the information. (Note: other free programs are also available online.)

2. Say to students, "Since this text is about culture, that word will be in the middle of our concept map."

3. Read through the text and discuss the outlying clusters for the map.

4. It is important to discuss how the clusters relate to the topic (religion to culture) and how the items in the cluster relate to each other (religion to beliefs).

Strategy *in Action*

Text

CULTURE

Culture is what makes people of different nationalities or geographical areas special. Culture is based on people's beliefs, religion, and nationality. It is the way humans live, which includes the food we eat, the makeup of our families, the way we dress, and even the games we play.

Culture is handed down from one generation to another. Family interaction and social gatherings help keep a culture alive. We continue with what we value and keep traditions that are meaningful to us.

Class Model

Directions for Independent Application

1. Once the model concept map is completed and students have no questions, assign the independent text.

2. Distribute blank pieces of paper to students on which they should write the main idea in a circle in the middle. Then they gather information for clusters as they read.

 ## Taking Ownership

Using webbing software, students type in the main ideas and details from their notes. They must also use arrows to show the connections and relationships between concepts.

 ## Assessment

When assessing students' concept maps, ask yourself the following:

✔ Is all the information correct?

✔ Are the best concepts represented?

✔ Are the concepts clustered together correctly?

 ## Differentiation

✦ To scaffold this task, place the assigned text's concepts into a premade concept map. Have students finish by adding details to the clusters.

✦ To extend this task, have students research in other texts for information that can be added to their basic concept map, and explain why this information should be added to the cluster.

 ## Variations

✦ Students make a concept map by putting the main ideas in one color and the supporting details in another. Text boxes can be used to keep words in clusters.

✦ Students use a collage of representative images to make a concept map. Students cut out pictures from magazines that represent the concepts, glue them into cluster groups, and label the clusters.

Lesson 23

Points With Evidence

 ## What Is It?

While reading a text, students look for evidence that supports the author's point. Students identify reasons behind what an author states. For example, if an author states that life does not exist on a planet, students would identify the reasons the author gives to support this point, such as that there is no air or water on the planet. Students write down the author's point and the reasons the author gives for making the statement. Explain to students that the main idea can be stated explicitly by the author, or can be implied as a central thought. In this case, readers use points given by the author to form the main idea.

 ## Why Use It?

Authors consistently make points or "blanket" statements about various subjects. With reputable publishers and sources, we assume the author's point is accurate and based on sound reasoning. The Points With Evidence activity fosters students' ability to identify the reasons an author has stated to support his "blanket" statement or the point that he is making. Finding evidence to support a statement aligns with the Common Core standards and is used within strategies that foster close reading (Fisher and Frey, 2012). Identifying reasons for an author's statement begins the journey towards identifying points of view in essay writing or argumentation.

 ## Text Selection

To introduce this activity, choose an opinion text that is powerfully one-sided, for example, a text on why we should save our endangered species or whether we should allow the use of pesticides. The text must have evidence for points that are being made.

Instructional Steps

Introduction

1. Say to students, "Sometimes authors make a statement about a topic and the purpose of that statement is to make a point about the topic. For instance, an author might write that living in smog is unhealthy. Then the author usually gives several reasons that support this point, such as *smog is a combination of smoke and fog and it is unhealthy to breathe smoke,* or *smog can affect eyesight.*"

2. Discuss how the reasons given by the author seem very clear and support the point.

Strategy *in Action*

Text

BIGFOOT

Bigfoot are said to be large, hairy, ape-like creatures. Some people claim to have seen Bigfoot in the Pacific Northwest area of the United States. However, scientists say that Bigfoot do not exist. People who claim to have seen Bigfoot say that the creatures are between six and ten feet tall and look part ape and part human. Other people say Bigfoot is just folklore.

In 1958, a bulldozer operator had a friend make a cast of a Bigfoot footprint. But according to later newspaper accounts, this casting was all a hoax and the footprint was actually made by a local logger. Scientists say there is not enough food for a Bigfoot population to exist. Some people have shown pictures they have managed to take of what appears to be a Bigfoot, but scientists believe the images in these photographs are various animals with health problems, such as mange.

Class Model

Scientists say that Bigfoot do not exist.

- Story is folklore.
- Footprint was a hoax.
- Not enough food for a Bigfoot population.
- Pictures are different animals.

3. Explain to students that points made by authors are not necessarily the main idea or the author's purpose. For instance, in the example about smog, the main idea could be how to eliminate smog, and the author brings up the point that smog is unhealthy as a reason to get rid of smog. On the other hand, another author could write that smog is an unavoidable byproduct of jobs, which people need so they can afford to live and eat. Ask students if they think these points could also be acceptable.

Teacher Modeling and Guided Practice

1. Display a simple text in which the author has written a statement that makes a point.

2. Read the text and, with student input, recognize an author's point and the reasons the author has given to support this point.

3. On the board, write the author's point. Show students how to create a bulleted list of the reasons the author gives to support this point.

4. Discuss the relationship between the point and the reasons the author gives that support the point. Do they make sense? Are they logical and feasible? Could there be other reasons or something stated against the author's point?

Directions for Independent Application

1. Once students understand the procedure, assign the selected text.

2. As students read, they write down the author's point and underneath make a bulleted list of the reasons the author gives to support this point.

 Taking Ownership

In teams of two or three, students review the reasons they have selected as supporting evidence. Collaboratively, they discuss each reason and describe how the evidence supports the author's statement.

 Assessment

When assessing students' bulleted lists of evidence, ask yourself the following:

✔ Is the author's point or statement included?

✔ Are an appropriate number of reasons identified correctly?

✔ Are the reasons given as evidence stated correctly?

Differentiation

✦ To scaffold this task, discuss with students the point the author is making. Direct them to write this point down on a piece of paper. As they read the selection, have them independently create a bulleted list of the supporting reasons.

✦ To extend this task, after students have written the list the author's reasons, have them answer the following: Do the author's reasons make sense? Explain why or why not.

Variations

✦ Reverse the procedure to ensure students' understand what an author's point is. Give students a list of bulleted reasons and have them write a point that the author could be making.

✦ After students write the point and bulleted reasons, they write a counterpoint. For instance, in a text about Jupiter not being able to support life, students could write a counterpoint that a different type of living beings than what is found on Earth could exist on Jupiter.

Lesson 24

Sticky Questions

 ## What Is It?

In this activity, students write down three different questions as they read. On sticky notes students write: (1) one question for clarification of the text, (2) one question for clarification about a visual in the text, and (3) one recall question using information from the text and a visual that the group must answer.

 ## Why Use It?

While some students are able to use a visual, such as a graph, to clarify information, others may have trouble understanding them. According to Fisher, Frey, and Lapp (2008), students often don't know how to interpret visuals or when to make use of them. Teachers need to model the use of visuals so students can gain independence in this skill. The purpose of this activity is to help students understand that words in the text and visuals are meant to support each other. Students write questions that will help clarify information in order to deepen comprehension.

 ## Text Selection

Choose a text with graphics that support the narrative. The text structure is not important, but clearly written text will aid the reader in writing effective questions.

 ## Instructional Steps

Introduction

1. Discuss with students how visuals in a text help with understanding information in a text.

2. Explain to students that they need to understand how to interpret the information of different kinds of visuals.

Teacher Modeling and Guided Practice

1. Share a graph and table with students and discuss how to read the information.

2. Project a text that features visuals, such as graphs or tables, that support the information in the text. You can use the sample text.

3. Do a think-aloud with students. Discuss the text and the visuals. On a sticky note, write one clarifying question about the text and use a second sticky note for a question about a visual. Place these sticky notes on the text where the questions were generated.

4. On a third sticky note, write a factual question that students can answer directly from either the text or the visual.

Strategy *in Action*

Text

TOP TEN U.S. EXPORTED PRODUCTS IN 2012

Exported products aid our economy. When people in other nations buy our products, more jobs are created in the United States. According to the U.S. Bureau of Economics, the three largest export products from the United States in 2012 were computers and electronics equipment, chemicals, and machinery. Computers and electronics equipment makes up 18.5 percent of our exports, machinery makes up 18 percent, and chemicals 13.1 percent.

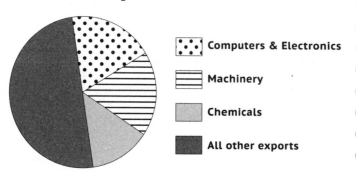

- Computers & Electronics
- Machinery
- Chemicals
- All other exports

Class Model

Sticky Note Questions

1. How do exports create jobs?

2. Why do the Machinery and Computer and Electronics pieces of the pie graph look the same size?

3. Which type of product was exported the most in 2012?

Directions for Independent Application

1. For this activity, students work in pairs. Give each pair three sticky notes. As students read, they write the questions on the sticky notes.

2. Students write one question to help clarify the text and place the sticky note in the text by information that prompted their question.

3. Students write down the next question to help clarify a visual and place the sticky note near the visual.

4. Finally, students make up one question about information in the text to see if another pair can find the answer in the text.

 ## Taking Ownership

Students share questions collaboratively in groups of four. Students should aid each other on the clarification questions and refer to the text if they cannot clarify those issues. For the recall question, the student who asks the question writes down the groups' answer; these can be collected for evaluation.

 ## Assessment

When assessing students' questions, ask yourself the following:

✔ Is the question relevant to the text or visual?

✔ Does the question make sense with the content being read?

✔ Are students able to correctly answer the recall question in the collaborative groups?

 ## Differentiation

✦ To scaffold this task, preview the selection with students. Do a feature walk, reading all bold text, headings, and vocabulary, and discuss the information contained in the visuals. Then assign the Sticky Questions.

✦ To extend this task, have students draw upon information from another source that relates to the same content and offers different visuals. Students then explain which visual helped them the most in understanding the content.

 ## Variations

✦ Students write questions about a topic prior to reading. They look through multiple sources to find the answers from the text and visuals.

✦ Assign students partners and have them answer each others' Sticky Questions.

RI.3.8   RI.4.8   RI.5.8

Points of Persuasion

What Is It?

Students are directed in this activity to look for points and visuals that could convince a person to choose one side of an issue over another (such as to use a particular type of lightbulb). Students read a selection that compares and contrasts two sides of a topic enabling them to see both sides of an issue. Students use a T-chart to write down the points the author states about each side of the issue.

Why Use It?

It is important that students be able to recognize when an author is writing objectively about different sides of an issue. The text structure usually used to show different sides of an issue is compare and contrast. This differs from persuasive writing, in which an author presents persuasive points about one position. Text structure influences a reader's comprehension and changes conceptual beliefs in readers (Kendeou, Muis, and Fulton, 2011). Students need to understand the two sides of an issue to form opinions or make decisions that can affect their life or beliefs. Giving students strategies for how to focus on reasons or points stated for each side of an issue aids in their decision making.

Text Selection

Choose a text that objectively compares and contrasts two sides of an issue or event. The text should be about a subject that is presented fairly and written by an unbiased source.

Instructional Steps

Introduction

1. Ask students, "Have you ever had to choose between buying one toy or video game over another?" Ask someone to share what one game offered and compare this to what the other game offered.

2. Write these points on a T-chart. Ask students to evaluate the information on the T-chart and discuss how they would come to a decision about which game to purchase.

3. Discuss how authors present reasons when they are writing about two different sides of an issue. For instance, if we were to write about getting an extra recess, we could talk about gaining social time and more exercise. But, by contrast, not having an extra recess could provide more group learning time and more time exercise our brains. Explain that authors often write about two different sides of an issue so readers can understand the content more clearly and can make better decisions.

Teacher Modeling and Guided Practice

1. Show students a text that compares and contrasts an issue or topic.

2. Project the reading material and draw a T-chart on the board or chart paper.

3. Prior to writing on the chart, read the entire text with students.

4. Ask them to identify what is being compared and contrasted and label the top of the T-chart with the topics.

5. Read through the piece again and show students how they can find reasons or points that the author gives about the topic. Write the appropriate facts on both sides of the chart. (As students get more comfortable with the process, have them identify the facts.)

6. Discuss how the author uses these points to explain the content.

Directions for Independent Application

1. Students create a T-chart to use with their assigned reading.

2. Remind them to read through the text first, and then reread to find the topics and points to write on the T-chart.

Strategy *in Action*

Text

GENETICALLY ALTERED FOOD

Did you know that some of our food is genetically altered? This means that scientists combine genes and add proteins from other living things to change a plant. Sometimes this new combination helps the plant become more resistant to harmful insects. Sometimes the new combination helps the fruit or vegetable to grow bigger than it normally would. Sometimes the new combination makes the fruit or vegetable grow faster. This helps farmers to make more food for the world.

On the other hand, many people buy only organic fruits and vegetables. You may have seen a sign in your grocery store that says, "Organic." This means that the fruits and vegetables may not have any new combinations of genes and do not get fertilized with anything that might pollute the earth. Organic farmers rotate their plants so nutrients in the soil are not used up. Some people feel that organic food is safer to eat.

Class Model

GENETICALLY ALTERED FOOD	ORGANIC FOOD
Combined genes and added proteins change plant	May not have combined genes and added proteins
Plants more resistant to insects	Farmers rotate plants for better soil
Bigger fruits and vegetables	No pollution
Grow faster	Safer to eat
More food for world	

Taking Ownership

Place students into pairs and have each student choose a different side of the issue. Using the notes from the T-chart, students discuss the issue and try to persuade each other to support their side of the issue. Students then discuss the reasons the author might have had for making certain points and not others.

Assessment

When assessing students' T-charts, ask yourself the following:

✔ Have both sides of the issue been identified correctly?

✔ Does the T-chart have accurate information?

✔ Is the information on the T-chart complete?

Differentiation

◆ To scaffold this task, help students label the two sides of the T-chart. If needed, guide students through filling out one side of the T-chart and have them work with a partner to complete the second side.

◆ To extend this task, have students add to the T-chart. Underneath each reason, students give the reason a 1 to 5 rating, 1 being weak, 5 being strong. Students discuss with a partner why they gave each rating.

Variations

◆ If there are overlapping reasons within the two issues, students use a Venn diagram instead of a T-chart.

◆ Instead of using a T-chart, students use a three-column chart. Students write the two sides of the issue in the first two columns and create a third stance for the third column. After taking notes on the reasons given for the first two sides, they describe reasons for the third stance.

It's All in How You SLICE It!

 What Is It?

As students read, they use the It's All in How You SLICE It! graphic organizer to take notes. The SLICE acronym stands for the following:

S = *Summarize* points while reading.
L = *List* important ideas and words.
I = Write down where there is *inadequate information*.
C = Write a *conversation* point from a graphic.
E = Write an *example that explains* something within the text.

 Why Use It?

SLICE gives students the opportunity to interact with the text by writing summary points from both text and graphics. It has been well documented that the use of summarizing as a strategy increases understanding (McKeown, Beck, and Blake, 2009). Allowing students to take guided notes during reading aids them in going directly to the meaning of the text. McKeown, Beck, and Blake also found that strategy instruction does not necessarily build meaning for students, rather students need to attend to the text content by focusing on important ideas and relationships between ideas. The SLICE activity helps student use the text and text features to focus on important ideas, which increases their understanding and retention of information in the text.

 Text Selection

Texts for this activity must contain graphics. Since the C is for *conversation point from a graphic*, it's best to select texts which have highly informative graphics. For instance, a graph depicting petroleum use in different countries will lead to a much deeper conversation than just a picture of oil wells.

Instructional Steps

Introduction

1. Share with students the It's All in How You SLICE It! graphic organizer and explain that the acronym represents different tasks that they will complete as they read. Say to students, "Each letter represents something you need to do as you read."

2. "The *S* stands for *summarize points*. This means that you summarize bits of what the author is saying."

3. "The *L* stands for *list important ideas*. This means that you list something important or give a definition if the author writes one in the text."

4. "The *I* stands for *inadequate information*. This is something you want to know more about, so most likely you will write a question here."

5. "The *C* stands for a *conversation point from a graphic*. Find something you'd like to discuss about a graphic that is in the text. For instance, if there is a graph, you might write down something interesting you learned from the graph to share with your group."

6. "The *E* stands for an *example or explanation*. An author will add information so readers can understand something better. This would be an example or explanation."

Teacher Modeling and Guided Practice

1. Using a sample text, go through each letter step with students.

2. Be sure that students understand the *C* pertains to the visuals within the text.

Directions for Independent Application

1. Distribute copies of the It's All in How You SLICE It! graphic organizer.

2. Students complete the graphic organizer as they read their assigned text.

3. Remind them that the *C* is for a *conversation point from a graphic* in the text.

Text

BATTLE OF BUNKER HILL

The Revolutionary War was fought between the American colonies and England in order for the colonists to gain their freedom from England. One important battle fought during that war, called the Battle of Bunker Hill, took place on June 13, 1775. The battle was supposed to take place on Bunker Hill, but actually took place on nearby Breed's Hill. Although the soldiers were supposed to fight on the 110-foot-high Bunker Hill, the officers decided to fight on the 62-foot-high Breed's Hill because it was closer to Boston. Today, the Bunker Hill Monument is actually on top of Breed's Hill.

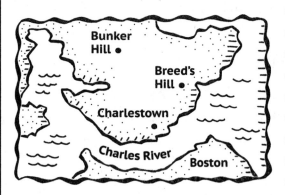

Class Model

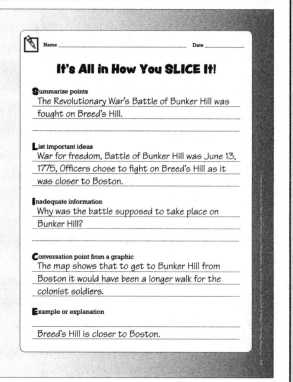

Name _____ Date _____

It's All in How You SLICE It!

Summarize points
The Revolutionary War's Battle of Bunker Hill was fought on Breed's Hill.

List important ideas
War for freedom, Battle of Bunker Hill was June 13, 1775, Officers chose to fight on Breed's Hill as it was closer to Boston.

Inadequate information
Why was the battle supposed to take place on Bunker Hill?

Conversation point from a graphic
The map shows that to get to Bunker Hill from Boston it would have been a longer walk for the colonist soldiers.

Example or explanation

Breed's Hill is closer to Boston.

Taking Ownership

Place students in groups of three or four. Each student shares the information written on the graphic organizer. Students refer to the visual from the text when they are sharing their conversation point so the group will know which visual this information came from.

Assessment

When assessing students' graphic organizers, ask yourself the following:

✔ Have the SLICE categories been filled out correctly?

✔ Is all the information correct?

✔ Does the visual portray the information given by the student for *C*, the conversation point?

Differentiation

✦ To scaffold this task, review the graphic organizer with students. Have students work in pairs to list summary points and the important facts. Then have them complete the rest independently.

✦ To extend this task, have students research to find the answer to the question they wrote for "Inadequate information." Allow them to share this answer with the group or class.

Variations

✦ Use the SLICE formula for text that does not contain any graphics. Have the "C" represent a conversation point from the text.

✦ Turn SLICE into SLICED. Using their informational notes, students *draw* a graphic that supports or expands on information in the text.

It's All in How You SLICE It!

Summarize points

_____

_____

_____

List important ideas

_____

_____

_____

Inadequate information

_____

_____

_____

Conversation point from a graphic

_____

_____

_____

Example or explanation

_____

_____

RI.3.8 RI.4.8 RI.5.8

Think-Pair-Share

 ## What Is It?

In this collaborative reflection activity, students read with partners using the Think-Pair-Share strategy. You can mark stopping spots in the text or allow students to decide how much to read prior to stopping for discussion. The stopping spots should be at the end of a section or page. At each selected stop, students discuss their thoughts about the material read. They continue reading once they both agree they are ready.

 ## Why Use It?

Although the Think-Pair-Share strategy is often used in the classroom to allow students to interact with material being presented, it is not as commonly used in reading. When students stop, think, and talk about the text, they are able to clarify understanding and build deeper meaning of the text. According to Arrequín-Anderson and Esquiredo (2011), the dyad strategy (partnership) of Think-Pair-Share increases the cognitive engagement of students and allows them to process information better. Through collaboration and verbal interaction, students are able to engage with the information, clarify, and expand understanding as they discuss it with partners. A supportive classroom context includes high-quality talk about text, not just from teacher to student but from student to student (Duke and Pearson, 2008). Think-Pair-Share allows students to talk about the text at various levels, from clarification of concepts to individual word meanings.

 ## Text Selection

The text for this activity should have easily recognizable stopping points. This could be at a particular bold heading or when a topic ends on a particular page. Initially, choosing a shorter selection will make it easier for you to teach students how to identify sections and discuss information with their partners.

Introduction

1. Review Think-Pair-Share with students; they may know this as a "Turn and Talk." Explain to students that they are going to do a Think-Pair-Share as they read.

2. Explain what students might want to discuss with their partner, such as asking a question, making a connection, or giving more information about the topic.

Strategy *in Action*

Text

PHOTOSYNTHESIS

Photosynthesis is how plants make their own food. The sun provides the necessary light plants need to make food. Plants also use carbon dioxide, which is what we breathe out! Finally, plants also need water to help make their food.

Plants are made of tiny cells. Inside the cells are tiny chloroplasts. Chloroplasts take the light from the sun, the carbon dioxide from the air, and use water to make food for the plant. Then the plant releases oxygen for us to breathe.

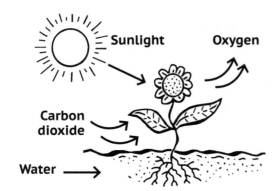

Class Model

> Think-Pair-Share Notes
>
> Jermaine and I discussed the picture in the book because I was confused about the oxygen. I didn't know that plants make oxygen for us to breathe.

Teacher Modeling and Guided Practice

1. Ask someone in class to be your partner to model the Think-Pair-Share for reading.

2. Using a sample text, point out to your partner where the first reading stop will be. Tell the class that for the purpose of demonstration you are going to read the text orally so all can hear.

3. Stop at your designated spot and discuss the reading with your partner. You can model by saying something like, "I understood all that I read so far, but I'm not sure I understand why the author put this picture on the page." Let your partner model how he would respond to that. Continue modeling through a short text.

4. Model for students how you would write up notes about your discussion, pointing out how your partner clarified something for you or made you think differently about what you read.

Directions for Independent Application

1. Place students in pairs and assign the intended reading.

2. Designate stopping spots or let students decide when they should stop and discuss.

3. After students do the Think-Pair-Share with their partner, they will write notes about what took place during their discussion.

 ## Taking Ownership

After reading, partners reflect on their discussion by writing what they have learned from each other. This can be done solo or completed with partners. Partners write and explain how parts of their discussion helped them understand the text or think differently about it.

 ## Assessment

When assessing students' Think-Pair-Share notes, ask yourself the following:

✔ Does the written reflection portray correct information?

✔ Does the reflection include an example from the partner discussion?

✔ Does the written reflection show understanding of the information?

Differentiation

✦ To scaffold this task, allow students to discuss orally with you the areas in the text that were confusing.

✦ To extend this task, do a Think-Pair-Square. After partners have discussed their thoughts about the text, "square" partners with another set of partners for groups of four. Have the group discuss the reading and share an important piece of their learning with the class.

 Variations

✦ Partners set up for a Think-Pair-Share and preview the text together before reading. Instruct students to look over the bold words and graphics and discuss what the text might be about. Then have students read and conduct the Think-Pair-Share.

✦ Add visualization to the Think-Pair-Share. Give students designated places in the text to stop and draw a graphic that explains what they just read. Partners stop to share and discuss their visualizations as part of their conversation. Continue to the end of the text.

Lesson 28

Free-Thinking Sticky Notes

 ## What Is It?

The focus of this activity is to support students as they read two texts on the same topic. Students are not given a specific purpose for writing on the sticky notes. The sole direction given is to write a certain number of thoughts on sticky notes for each of the texts assigned. A different color sticky note should be used with each text. For instance, yellow sticky notes may be used while reading the first book, and green sticky notes used with the second book. When the readings are complete the sticky notes will be discussed with a small group.

 ## Why Use It?

Using sticky notes to write down free thoughts allows students to think about a topic in a natural, interactive manner. Activities that generate connections from what students know to other content allows students to gain deep understanding of content (McNamara, 2011). As students write thoughts, these notes will naturally fall into categories such as connections, questions, clarifications, and explanations—all interactions that foster deeper comprehension. When reading multiple texts on the same topic, students need to use more strategic effort than when trying to understand a single text on one topic (Bråten, Britt, Strømsø, and Rouet, 2011). Writing thoughts on sticky notes supports students as they engage with the content in two texts. Discussion, stemming from the sticky note comments, will aid students in their construction of meaning as they combine ideas from the two different texts.

 ## Text Selection

Select two books on the same topic that contain different information. Although some content of the books may overlap, each should support or contrast and expand information on the topic.

Strategy *in Action*

Text 1

Frogs are amphibians. This means that frogs begin their life in the water and then live on land. Frogs start their life in the water as eggs, which grow into tadpoles. Tadpoles live in the water until they fully develop into frogs.

Text 2

Frogs are amphibians because they live in water, then on land. This is because they start life as a tadpole and change into a frog. This is called metamorphosis. Metamorphosis means changing from one thing into another. Some animals change in different stages of their life. The frog eggs become tadpoles, then the tadpoles change into froglets, and finally the froglets change into fully developed frogs. In the tadpole and froglet stages, the animal has a tail, but the tail disappears and lungs develop in the full grown frog.

Class Model

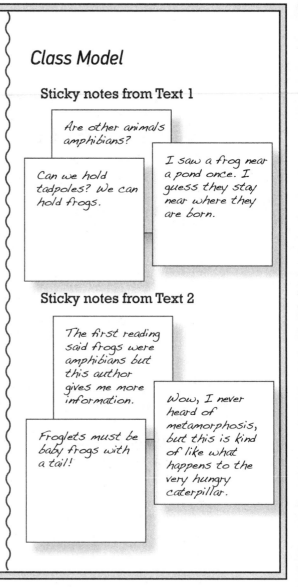

Sticky notes from Text 1

Are other animals amphibians?

Can we hold tadpoles? We can hold frogs.

I saw a frog near a pond once. I guess they stay near where they are born.

Sticky notes from Text 2

The first reading said frogs were amphibians but this author gives me more information.

Froglets must be baby frogs with a tail!

Wow, I never heard of metamorphosis, but this is kind of like what happens to the very hungry caterpillar.

 Instructional Steps

Introduction

1. Explain to students that they are going to read two different texts on the same subject.

2. Tell students they are going to write comments on a specific number of sticky notes as they read. The comments can be a note to remember information, questions, or various thoughts about the material read. When beginning this activity, give students a maximum of one sticky note per page.

Teacher Modeling and Guided Practice

1. Select two short texts on the same topic that offer complementary information.

2. Model for students by reading the first text. As you read, do a think-aloud and write your thoughts on sticky notes.

3. Read a second short text to students and continue with your think-aloud. When possible, make connections from the first reading to the second. Write down your thoughts on a different color of sticky notes in order to distinguish which text the thoughts came from.

4. If you are reading about volcanoes, you might say, "I never thought about volcanic ash staying in the air. I wonder if that can make us sick?"

5. Discuss your sticky notes with students and categorize them into connections, questions, clarifications, or explanations.

6. Look over the categories and decide if one of the texts led to a particular type of thought.

7. Ask students which text they preferred and why.

8. Ask if both texts helped them understand the topic better.

9. Explain that reading information from different sources helps us learn a lot more about something.

Directions for Independent Application

1. Give students two different color sticky notes and assign the texts.

2. Students write down thoughts from each text on the appropriate sticky notes.

3. When reading the second text, they make comparisons with the first one and explain what information is the same or different.

 Taking Ownership

Students meet in small groups to discuss the texts. Students discuss the sticky notes and talk about both texts. Then students categorize the group's sticky notes under different comprehension strategies: connections, questions, clarifications, or explanations. Students check the categorization to see if they need more clarification from one text or the other and discuss what this means about the text. Finally, student groups tell you which text they prefer and why.

Assessment

When assessing students' Free-Thinking Sticky Notes, ask yourself the following:

✔ Do the sticky notes contain pertinent information from the texts?

✔ Were all the sticky notes used effectively?

✔ Is it clear which text was preferred and why?

Differentiation

✦ To scaffold this task, have students read in pairs and discuss what might go on a sticky note prior to writing it. Then have partners write sticky notes when they both agree one is needed.

✦ To extend this task, give students a third reading and a third color of sticky notes. The group takes notes on and discusses all three texts.

Variations

✦ Give students a large, poster-size Venn diagram labeled with the names of the two texts. Students place their sticky notes in each text's circle or in the overlapping circle if the thought came from both texts.

✦ Divide students into two groups and give each one a different text to read. Each group discusses their sticky notes. Then put partners together from the two different groups. The new partners share their original group's discussion points.

Text One and Text Two

What Is It?

Using a three-column chart, students write important facts in the first column as they read "Text One," the first assigned reading. In the second column, students write important facts from "Text Two." Students should find facts in both the text and the graphics. Finally, students work in groups to identify and synthesize information from both texts to create a new understanding of the topic that they record in the third column.

Why Use It?

In Bloom's taxonomy (Eber and Parker, 2007), synthesizing information is considered a challenging task. Effective readers are able to synthesize information. Students need to be able to synthesize information from multiple texts both for academic purposes and as a life skill. When students synthesize, they integrate information from different sources, often multimodal, to increase understanding of a topic. Studies have found that reading multiple documents promotes deeper understanding and more interconnected understanding than reading just one text on the topic (Gil, Bråten, Vidal-Abarca, and Strømsø, 2010). Using the three-column chart scaffolds students as they learn to synthesize and combine information from multiple texts.

Text Selection

Select two texts on the same topic that contain different information. Although some content in the texts will overlap, it is best if the two texts support and expand on each other.

Strategy *in Action*

Text One

MARS

Mars is the fourth planet from the sun and is Earth's neighbor. Mars has a red tint because the surface of Mars has lots of the mineral iron oxide. It is like the color rust, with a reddish hue. Mars has frozen North and South poles just like Earth. Because of all the frozen water on Mars some scientist think life could have once existed there.

Text Two

MARS

Mars' nickname is the Red Planet because it looks red from a distance. Because Mars is relatively close to Earth, the United States has sent different spacecraft to explore Mars. The surface of Mars is dusty and rocky. Mars is a very cold planet, and there is no life there. It has very strong winds, which cause dangerous dust storms. Unlike Earth, Mars has two very small moons, instead of one.

Class Model

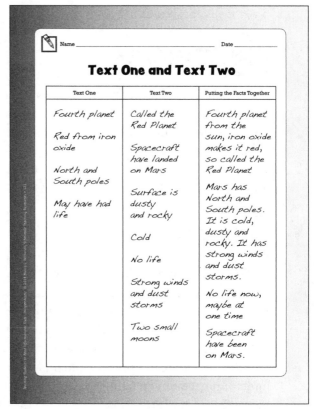

Name _____ Date _____

Text One and Text Two

Text One	Text Two	Putting the Facts Together
Fourth planet	Called the Red Planet	Fourth planet from the sun, iron oxide makes it red, so called the Red Planet
Red from iron oxide	Spacecraft have landed on Mars	
North and South poles	Surface is dusty and rocky	Mars has North and South poles. It is cold, dusty and rocky. It has strong winds and dust storms.
May have had life	Cold	
	No life	
	Strong winds and dust storms	No life now, maybe at one time
	Two small moons	Spacecraft have been on Mars.

⟳ Instructional Steps

Introduction

1. Explain to students that they are going to get information on the same topic from two different texts.

2. Tell students they will write notes so they can compare and combine the information from the two texts.

Teacher Modeling and Guided Practice

1. Select two short texts on the same topic that offer complementary information.

2. Display a three-column chart labeled with the headings "Text One," "Text Two," and "Putting the Facts Together."

3. Say to students, "We will be reading two texts and writing down important facts from both."

4. Read the first text with students and write down the important information in the corresponding column.

5. Do the same with the second text, having students help you identify the important information.

6. Read the title of the third column, "Putting the Facts Together," and ask students what they think it means. Then explain that you will be looking at columns one and two to come up with information to write in the third column.

7. Start with column one and read the first fact. Ask students if there is anything from Text Two that you could put together with it for the third column.

8. Discuss the information and explain how each piece tells us more about the topic. Write a sentence in the third column that integrates information from columns one and two.

9. Continue through all the facts this way. When you are finished with the first column, have students see if there is anything left in the second column that needs to be written in the "Putting the Fact Together" column.

Directions for Independent Application

1. Distribute copies of the Text One and Text Two graphic organizer.

2. Group students in pairs and give them the two assigned texts.

3. Students fill out the graphic organizer during reading.

Taking Ownership

After reading both texts, students work with a partner to discuss the important facts they have written down. Partners compare what they have written down and add more information if needed. Then students discuss how the information in each text differed and how having information from both texts increased their understanding.

Assessment

When assessing students' three-column charts, ask yourself the following:

✔ Do the columns from each text contain enough information?

✔ Is all the information correct?

✔ Is the information from each text synthesized appropriately?

Differentiation

✦ To scaffold this task, work with students on the first text. Have students work with a partner on the second text.

✦ To extend this task, have students write a summary using the information they synthesized in the third column.

Variations

✦ Students put the important facts from each text on sticky notes. Then they categorize the sticky notes into topics.

✦ Divide the work. Split the class or group into sections. Have one section read Text One and write down important facts. Have the second section read Text Two and write the important facts. Match a student from the Text One section with a student from the Text Two section and have them collaborate to put the information together.

Text One and Text Two

Text One	Text Two	Putting the Facts Together

Lesson 30

"Peer-amid" Points

 What Is It?

In the "Peer-amid" Points activity, students "peer" amid two different texts for factual information, then organize their notes from the two texts into four areas: topic, main ideas, important facts, and interesting facts. Using a pyramid shaped graphic organizer, students write the topic of the selection at the top of the pyramid. As they read, students summarize facts and evaluate the importance of those facts. The least important or interesting facts are placed at the bottom of the pyramid. The most important facts are written above the interesting facts, and above those, students list the main ideas.

 Why Use It?

Not all students easily acquire the skills needed to be effective readers and writers of informational text (Bass and Woo, 2008). When students write down main ideas and important facts they begin to paraphrase the author's language and use their own language. Translating written language into spoken language gives us understanding (Zhihui, 2008). Writing down information allows us to engage with the text differently. In addition, students need to learn to gather information from multiple sources. Integrating text information from more than one source is a necessary skill that deepens comprehension both for reading and for writing reports.

 Text Selection

Select two texts on the same topic that contain different information. Although some content of each text will overlap, the text information should support or contrast and expand information on the topic.

Strategy *in Action*

Text One

THE PURCHASE OF ALASKA

Russia owned the Alaskan territory and needed money. The Ambassador to Russia approached the U.S. Secretary of State, William H. Seward, about buying Alaska. Seward wanted the United States to buy Alaska and they agreed upon a price of $7.2 million. The purchase passed in the U.S. by only one vote. At that time, many people thought the Alaskan land was worthless.

Text Two

SEWARD'S FOLLY

Russia sold Alaska to the United States in 1867, shortly after the Civil War ended. The U.S. Secretary of State, William Seward, offered the price of $7.2 million. Much of Alaska had not been explored, and people thought the land was worthless. So, Alaska's purchase became known as Seward's Folly. The definition of *folly* is a foolish act or idea. It is now said that Seward's Folly is one of the best purchases the United States ever made.

Class Model

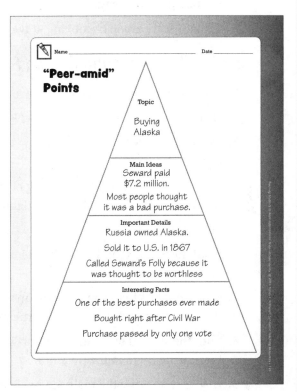

Name _____ Date _____

"Peer-amid" Points

Topic
Buying Alaska

Main Ideas
Seward paid $7.2 million.
Most people thought it was a bad purchase.

Important Details
Russia owned Alaska.
Sold it to U.S. in 1867
Called Seward's Folly because it was thought to be worthless

Interesting Facts
One of the best purchases ever made
Bought right after Civil War
Purchase passed by only one vote

⟳ Instructional Steps

Introduction

1. Tell students that the word *peer* means "to look intently."
2. When we read two texts for information, we must "peer," or look intently, at what the books have to say.
3. Explain that we will be looking at two texts to gather information on one topic.

Teacher Modeling and Guided Practice

1. Select two short texts on the same topic that offer complementary information.
2. Display an enlarged version of the "Peer-Amid" Points graphic organizer.
3. Say to students, "We will be reading two texts and writing down information from both."
4. Explain that while you are reading everyone should be reading or listening for the main ideas, important details, and interesting facts.
5. Discuss the topic of the texts and write that at the top of the pyramid.
6. Read the first text and write down important details and interesting facts as you read.
7. Have students help you identify the main idea(s) from the selection and write those in the main idea section of the pyramid.
8. With the second text, have students identify the important details and interesting facts. Write them in the pyramid.
9. Discuss and write the main idea(s) from the second reading.
10. Discuss how reading two different texts about the same topic helps us gain more knowledge and understanding about a topic.

Directions for Independent Application

1. Distribute copies of the "Peer-Amid" Points graphic organizer.
2. Explain to students how they will work with two texts.
3. Students fill in the graphic organizer as they read each selection.

Taking Ownership

Students work in small groups to compare the information they have written from each text. They discuss how the two texts gave them more knowledge than reading just one text.

Assessment

When assessing students' "Peer-amid" Points graphic organizer, ask yourself the following:

✔ Do the sections on the pyramid contain information from both texts?

✔ Is all the information correct?

✔ Is the information from each text integrated correctly?

Differentiation

✦ To scaffold this task, work with students to identify the topic and main ideas. Have them work with partners to complete the pyramid.

✦ To extend this task, have students go online to research more information about the topic. Have them add the information from a third source to the pyramid.

Variations

✦ Students use a three-dimensional pyramid form. (Do an online search for three-dimensional pyramid pattern and you will find various sites with patterns.) Students write the pyramid information on the four sides of the pyramid. They use one side for the topic, one for the main idea(s), one for the important facts, and the last side for the interesting facts.

✦ Use multimodal sources instead of two written texts. Show students a short video or PowerPoint on a topic and have them read a text. Students fill out the graphic organizer using information from both sources.

"Peer-amid" Points

Topic

Main Ideas

Important Details

Interesting Facts

References

Amiryousefi, M., & Ketabi, S. (2011). Mnemonic instruction: A way to boost vocabulary learning and recall. *Journal of Language Teaching & Research, 2*(1), 178–182. doi:10.4304/jltr.2.1.178-182

Arreguín-Anderson, M., & Esquierdo, J. (2011). Overcoming difficulties. *Science & Children, 48*(7), 68–71.

Bass, M., & Woo, D. (2008). Comprehension Windows Strategy: A comprehension strategy and prop for reading and writing informational text. *Reading Teacher, 61*(7), 571–575. doi:10.1598/RT.61.7.7

Baumann, J. F., & Graves, M. F. (2010). What is academic vocabulary? *Journal of Adolescent & Adult Literacy, 54*(1), 4–12. doi:10.1598/JAAL.54.1.1

Beck, I. L., McKeown, M. G., & Kucan, L. (2002). *Bringing words to life: Robust vocabulary instruction.* New York: Guilford.

Bintz, W. P. (2011). Teaching vocabulary across the curriculum. *Middle School Journal, 42*(4), 44–53.

Block, C. C., & Duffy, G. G. (2008). Research on teaching comprehension: Where we've been and where we're going. In C. C. Block & S. R. Paris (Eds.), *Comprehension instruction: Research based best practices* (2nd ed., pp. 19–37). New York: Guilford.

Bluestein, N. (2010). Unlocking text features for determining importance in expository text: A strategy for struggling readers. *Reading Teacher, 63*(7), 597–600.

Boulware, B. J., & Crow, M. (2008). Using the concept attainment strategy to enhance reading comprehension. *Reading Teacher, 61*(6), 491–495.

Bråten, I., Britt, M. A., Strømsø, H. I., & Rouet, J. F. (2011). The role of epistemic beliefs in the comprehension of multiple expository texts: towards an integrated model. *Educational Psychologist, 46*, 48–70.

Carmelina Films (Producer). (2009). *Blogging in the classroom* [video]. (Available from Films Media Group, New York, NY.)

Coleman, J., Bradley, L. & Donovan C. (2012). Visual representations in second graders' information book compositions. *Reading Teacher, 66*(1), 31–45. Newark, NJ: International Reading Association.

Cummins, S, & Stallmeyer-Gerard, C. (2001). *Reading Teacher, 64*(6), 394–405. doi:10.1598/RT.64.6.1

Daly, A., & Unsworth, L. (2011). Analysis and comprehension of multimodal texts. *Australia Journal of Language & Literacy, 34*(1), 61–80.

Duke, N. K., & Pearson, P. (2008). Effective practices for developing reading comprehension. *Journal of Education, 189*(1/2), 107–122.

Eber, P. A. and Parker, T. S. (2007). Assessing student learning: Applying Bloom's taxonomy. *Human Service Education, 27*(1), 45–53.

Fink, R. (2011). Read, write, rap, rhyme. *New England Reading Association Electronic Newsletter, 3*(1), 4–5.

Fisher, D. and Frey, N. (2012). Close reading in elementary schools. *The Reading Teacher 66*(3), 179–188.

Fisher, D., Lapp, D., & Wood, K. (2011). Reading for details in online and printed text: A prerequisite for deep reading. *Middle School Journal. 42*(3), 58–63.

Fisher, D., Frey, N., & Lapp, D. (2008). Shared readings: modeling comprehension, vocabulary, text structures, and text features for older readers. *Reading Teacher, 61*(7), 548–556. doi:10.1598/RT.61.7.4

Gil, L., Bråten, I., Vidal-Abarca, E., & Strømsø, H. I. (2010). Understanding and integrating multiple science texts: Summary tasks are sometimes better than argument tasks. *Reading Psychology, 31*(1), 30–68. doi:10.1080/02702710902733600

Gomez, L., Herman, P., & Gomez, K. (2007). Integrating text in content-area classes: Better supports for teachers and students. *Voices in Urban Education, 14*(Winter), 22–29.

Grabe, W., & Stoller, F. L. (2001). Reading for academic purposes: Guidelines for the ESL/EFL teacher. In M. Celce-Murcia (Ed.), *Teaching English as a second or foreign language* (pp. 187–203). Boston: Heinle & Heinle.

Graham, S., & Hebert, M. (2010). Writing to read: Evidence for how writing can improve reading (*A Carnegie Corporation Time to Act Report*). Washington, D.C.: Alliance for Excellent Education.

Keene, E. (2008). *To understand: New horizons in reading comprehension.* Portsmouth, NH: Heinemann.

Kelley, M. J., & Clausen-Grace, N. (2010). Guiding students through expository text with text feature walks. *Reading Teacher, 64*(3), 191–195. doi:10.1598/RT.64.3.4

Kendeou, P., Muis, K. R., & Fulton, S. (2011). Reader and text factors in reading comprehension processes. *Journal of Research in Reading, 34*(4), 365–383. doi:10.1111/j.1467-9817.2010.01436.x

Leopold, C., & Leutner, L. (2012). Science text comprehension: Drawing, main idea selection and summarizing as learning strategies. *Learning and Instruction, 22*(1), 16–26.

Magnifico, A. M. (2010). Writing for whom? Cognition, motivation, and a writer's audience. *Educational Psychologist, 45*(3), 167–184.

Marinak, B. (2008). Teaching the predictable nature of informational text. *CEDER Yearbook,* 15–26.

McKeown, M. G., Beck, I. L., & Blake, R. K. (2009). Rethinking reading comprehension instruction: a comparison of instruction for strategies and content approaches. *Reading Research Quarterly, 44*(3), 218–253.

McNamara, D. (2011). Measuring deep, reflective comprehension and learning strategies: challenges and successes. *Metacognition & Learning, 6*(2), 195–203. doi:10.1007/s11409-011-9082-8

Meyer, B. F., & Ray, M. N. (2011). Structure strategy interventions: Increasing reading comprehension of expository text. *International Electronic Journal of Elementary Education, 4*(1), 127–152.

Mills, K. A. (2009). Floating on a sea of talk: Reading comprehension through speaking and listening. *Reading Teacher, 63*(4), 325–329.

Pearson, P. D. and Gallagher, M. C. (1983). The instruction of reading comprehension. *Contemporary Educational Psychology, 8,* 317–344.

Rahmani, M. & Sadeghi, K. (2011). Effects of note-taking training on reading comprehension and recall. *Reading Matrix: An International Online Journal, 11*(2), 116–128.

Raphael, T. E., & Au, K. H. (2006). *QAR now: Question answer relationships.* New York: Scholastic.

Ray, M. N., & Meyer, B. F. (2011). Individual differences in children's knowledge of expository text structures: A review of literature. *International Electronic Journal of Elementary Education, 4*(1), 67–82.

Read, S., Reutzel, D. D., & Fawson, P. (2008). Do you want to know what I learned? Using informational trade books as models to teach text structure. *Early Childhood Education Journal, 36*(3), 213–219. doi:10.1007/s10643-008-0273-0

Ropič, M., & Aberšek, M. (2012). Web graphic organizers as an advanced strategy for teaching science textbook reading comprehension. *Problems of Education in the 21st Century, 41,* 87–99.

Ruurs, M. (2011). Acrostics are awesome! *Reading Today, 28*(6), 38.

Scruggs, T. E., Mastropieri, M. A., Berkeley, S. L., & Marshak, L. (2010). Mnemonic strategies: Evidence-based practice and practice-based evidence. *Intervention in School & Clinic, 46*(2), 79–86. doi:10.1177/1053451210374985

Sadler, C. R. (2011). Concept/definition maps to comprehend curriculum content. *Reading Teacher, 65*(3), 211–213. Adapted from *Comprehension Strategies for Middle Grade Learners.* doi:10.1002/TRTR.01029

Stahl, K., & Bravo, M. A. (2010). Contemporary classroom vocabulary assessment for content areas. *Reading Teacher, 63*(7), 566–578.

Szabo, S. (2008). Patterned poetry writing helps preservice teachers summarize content learning. *Delta Kappa Gamma Bulletin, 75*(1), 23–26.

Taboada, A., Bianco, S., & Bowerman, V. (2012). Text-based questioning: A comprehension strategy to build English language learners' content knowledge. *Literacy Research and Instruction, 51*(2), 87–109.

Taboada, A., & Guthrie, J. T. (2006). Contributions of student questioning and prior knowledge to construction of knowledge from reading information text. *Journal of Literacy Research, 38*(1), 1–35.

Williams, J. P., Hall, K. M., Lauer, K. D., Stafford, K. B., DeSisto, L. A., & de Cani, J. S. (2005). Expository text comprehension in the primary grade classroom. *Journal of Educational Psychology, 97*(4), 538–550.

Williams, J. P., Stafford, K., Lauer, K. D., Hall, K. M., & Pollini, S. (2009). Embedding reading comprehension training in content-area instruction. *Journal of Educational Psychology, 101*(1), 1–20. doi:10.1037/a0013152

Zhihui, F. (2008). Going beyond the fab five: Helping students cope with the unique linguistic challenges of expository reading in intermediate grades. *Journal of Adolescent & Adult Literacy, 51*(6), 476–487.